THE SOUTHERN W...5

C000220619

CONTENTS

© Kevin Robertson (Noodle Books) and the various contributors 2014
ISBN 978-1-909328-10-5
First published in 2014 by Kevin Robertson
under the **NOODLE BOOKS** imprint
PO Box 279
Corhampton
SOUTHAMPTON
SO32 3ZX
www.noodlebooks.co.uk
editorial@thesouthernway.co.uk

Printed in England by
Berforts Information Press Ltd.

Editorial

So 25 issues on - actually it is of course 26 as there was also the 'Preview'. With a bit of tweaking along the way we are still here and I sincerely hope likely to be for some time to come.

I recall being asked early on as to how many issues there would likely be? My response, perhaps more in anticipation than fact, was 'it will just keep going'. That is what I had hoped and indeed has proven to be the case, so a very big thank-you to all who have made it possible.

I will not comment upon milestones in this issue, we have done so several times in the past. Instead I will briefly say 'thank you' to all for their support over previous editions and indeed into the future – the latter a comment to those who have taken out subscriptions for future volumes.

So, a simple question, where do we go from here? In short, I suspect the answer is 'more of the same'. The fact that readership has remained constant for some time tells me what I need to know. I am not a believer in change for change sake, although sharp-eyed readers will note the 'tweak' to the style of numbering used on the cover – normal service will be resumed next time!

What I do not intend to do is fill each issue with anniversary articles, '103¼ years since…..', that is not what I believe you want, proving also I do take time to listen to views. As a result of this feedback some features have appeared less and others more. Articles are also always welcome, nay encouraged, but I will admit we do not take all that are offered. You have told me over the years what you like and equally what you do not, hence more of the same to come but I will also make no excuses for once in a while going 'off piste' but only occasionally.

You have told me what you like and also what is not so popular. It would be rude for the sake of the diligent work by the authors concerned to mention specific articles but I promise the message has been heard loud and clear.

It might then be appropriate to refer to some of the topics planned for the future which include (not necessarily in likely appearance order):

The rebuilding of the Bulleids – why certain locomotives were selected over others.
The SR Diesel Shunters.
The Kent Coal Fields
and of course more from Tony Carter, Jeremy Clarke, Terry Cole, Jeff Grayer, Graham Hatton, Mike King, Alan Postlethwaite 'et al' (and with apologies for anyone I have omitted to mention).

I should also state that Alan Blackburn has kindly agreed to continue with the late Tony Goodyear's major series on the History of the Southern Railway. Tony is sadly missed but it is some indication of the calibre of the man when we mention one of his last requests was for Alan to complete the work. Alan of course needs no separate introduction, his credibility will be known to nearly every reader.

I might also mention there will of course be more of the remarkable photographic collection from David Wallis in future issues, whilst another major feature will be the commencement of the memories of W Anderson. If not a name known to you, I promise it will be soon. (He was a Brighton Apprentice, preceded MacLeud on the IOW and went on to work at Southampton Control you will appreciate the importance and interest this will generate.)

As I mentioned at the beginning I am still also asked the question, 'How long will SW continue?' (not perhaps as frequently as during the early days but it still crops up from time to time). Well, we started in 2007, so including that first year 2014 is the eighth year of publication. We will continue until either you or I have had enough, I cannot say 'until I get a proper job', because I am one of those few fortunate individuals who has managed to turn a hobby and interest into a job. For being able to do so, I sincerely thank you all.

Finally, I recently had to travel on a 'Javelin' service to and from Ashford followed by Eurostar. to and from Paris. As the countryside rushed by at 100+mph, the mind could but slip back to what our forbears must have thought comparing each new technological move as it replaced the last. Ever larger steam engines, corridor coaches, electrification, modernisation, the list goes on. The trouble is we as humans have short memories, added to I feel it is also so vitally important to record the past rather than allow it to be forgotten. I like to think we as the present generation are more conscious of this responsibility than in the past. Hopefully SW is playing its own small part in so doing, and that is also due to you as contributors and readers alike.

Kevin Robertson

Front cover - Brighton. We counted seven different steam class on the shed and with at least two more in the background - plus a Southern Electric loco!

Opposite page - There was something about the Drummond T14 type that appeals to the eye, helped no doubt by the curving appearance of the smokebox saddle where it joins the cylinders. (An article on the class is planned for a future issue of 'SW'.) In the meanwhile we can do no better than illustrate No 444, recorded at Nine Elms on 16 July 1949, still with SR number and noticeably devoid of the front steam-heat pipe. No 444 had a further seven months of life and succumbed to withdrawal in February 1950. *C C B Herbert*

Pages 2/3 - Empty oil tanks for Fawley, approaching Swaythling.

Rear cover - Slumbering Fullerton - see pages 116 to 119. Stephen Duffell.

On 26th March 1959, U class Mogul no. 31799 heads a Waterloo-Basingstoke van train through Clapham Junction. The first vehicle is a Van C (BY in BR parlance), then a luggage van (PMV), followed by a GWR Fruit D, another Van C, three vanfits and at least six more utility vans at the rear – a typical Southern Region van train of the period.　　　　*F Hornby*

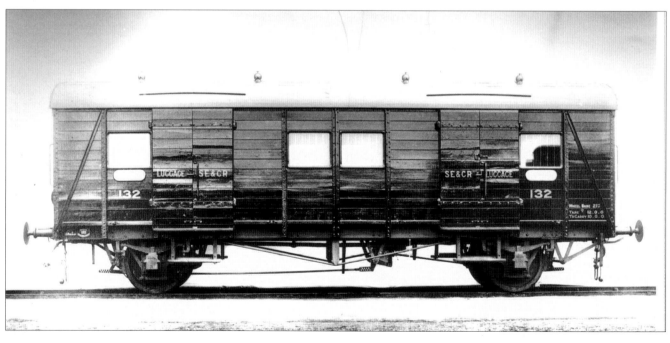

The prototype "Nurse Cavell van" when new at Ashford Works in April 1919, carrying SECR brown livery with yellow lettering. This is the livery now carried by the van as restored at Bodiam station on the KESR. Note the fact that only two destination slates (the grey coloured lozenge-shaped panels below the outer windows) are carried – later vans had these below all four side windows. The lack of ventilator hoods below the windows also characterises all pre-Grouping vans – compared with SR-built examples. Also the position of the vacuum cylinder varies from post-1923 construction.

SECR Official

VARIATIONS ON UTILITY VANS

Part 1: Pre-Grouping development and four-wheeled Covcars / Luggage Vans to 1939.

Mike King

The Southern's non-passenger coaching stock (often abbreviated to NPCS – vehicles built to run in passenger trains or at passenger train speeds without actually carrying passengers – to railwaymen they were often just "vans") largely comprises the family of vehicles known to us now as utility vans. This term comes from the first batch of covered carriage trucks (Covcars) built in 1928, which were actually labelled "General Utility Van" on their solebars, but this was not the origin of the design, even if perhaps the origin of the name.

The design dates back to SECR days – construction spanning 1919 until 1955 (with one additional rather curious rebuild that appeared in 1960) and in total comprised some 1988 vehicles – not that all were in service at the same time. The last examples were finally withdrawn from ordinary traffic in 1986 but some remain in departmental use to this day; giving a very respectable lifespan in excess of 90 years for the genre – and some might yet make it to a century! Even before Nationalisation they could be seen all over the country but with the general adoption of common user/go anywhere status for parcels vehicles since 1948, just about any van train might have included at least one in its make-up. Quite a number survive in preservation – most heritage railways each have more than one, but not all have been restored or returned to any form of service. Many are used as stores or workshop vans while others have been purchased for their underframes to be reused under pre-Grouping carriage bodies recovered from farms, beach huts, seaside bungalows and the like. Societies such as the Bluebell, the Kent and East Sussex and the Isle of Wight steam railway have all found them invaluable in this form, capable of combining a Victorian coach body with a suitable length underframe and modern running gear. Non-passenger coaching stock indeed! Some of the discarded van bodies now grace the trackside at these preserved lines as storage huts and very sturdy they prove in such a capacity.

To a large extent the design was fairly standardised – leading some to comment that they were all the same, but there was plenty of variation, as this series of articles will set out to prove.

Pre-Grouping development – the SECR vans

The story begins back in 1913, with the appointment of R E L Maunsell as CME to the South Eastern and Chatham Railway, replacing Harry Wainwright who departed from Ashford Works under something of a cloud. Maunsell found it necessary to recruit a completely new team and brought in Lionel Lynes (amongst others) from the GWR at Swindon, to become chief draughtsman with responsibility for carriages and wagons. A number of new wagon designs were then prepared, utilising RCH running gear combined with standardised steel channels and sections for the underframes and body skeleton. Amongst these was a 17ft long covered goods wagon with a rather distinctive semi-elliptical roof profile – soon to become familiar on the later SR vehicles. Constraints of wartime prevented much further progress but it was not a difficult matter to stretch the covered goods design to 32ft long (the length of other SECR six-wheeled passenger brake vans) and to produce a passenger luggage van with similar characteristics. The general arrangement drawing, dated January 1916, is reproduced here and carries the draughtsman's initials JRK (unknown) but checked by LL – quite obviously Lionel Lynes.

What was proposed was essentially a longer goods wagon rather than a shortened passenger coach – in marked contrast to most other British NPCS of the time, which tended to mirror the appearance of contemporary carriages. The drawing goes on to tell us that just one van (the "pattern" van) was to be built, for which purpose order number 308/18 (visible in the lower right-hand corner) was issued – the suffix 18 referring to the year of issue. The procedure of building a single prototype allowed any design improvements to be incorporated into the production models and was widely adopted by Maunsell and Lynes during the 1913-23 period. The prototype, SECR no. 132, was completed at Ashford in April 1919, carrying wartime brown livery with yellow lettering. Had pre-war conditions prevailed maybe the livery would have been crimson lake – as was applied to one of the Bluebell Railway vans a few years ago – possibly inaccurate but it certainly looked good. Just whether any of the production vehicles were so painted is unknown, but seeing Maunsell's views on locomotive liveries (a dull grey!) this is considered unlikely.

Only minor alterations were found to be needed on the production batches and a further 20 vans were then ordered from Bristol Wagon and Carriage Company. All bar one were delivered during August 1921, SECR numbers being 121-125 and 136-149. The last van, no. 150, was officially photographed by the builders in the following October, just prior to delivery. SR numbers of these were 1973-1992, the "pattern" van becoming SR number 1972. Twenty-four more came from Ashford Works between

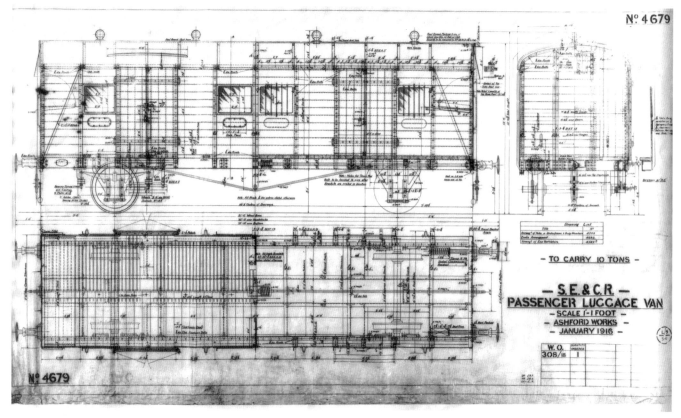

A copy of SECR general arrangement drawing no. 4679, dated January 1916, drawn by one JRK (initials) and checked by LL (Lionel Lynes). One van was ordered in 1918 but note that this drawing specifies destination slates below all four windows. There is a hinged shelf across each end of the van and a partition partway across on the centre-line. SR Diagram 960 faithfully records these details, neither of which was provided on SR-built vans to Diagram 3103.

August and October 1922, SECR numbers being 152-5/7/8/60-3/6-70/2-5/7/9-82. These later became SR numbers 1993-2016 after the Grouping. The Ashford batch differed in small details from the Bristol vans; the most obvious being the use of 'L' angles for the end uprights instead of "tee" sections on the Bristol batch. Most would have been employed on the South Eastern's more prestigious workings, including the Folkestone and Dover boat trains; however, the prototype van appears to have received special status during its first year or two.

The Nurse Cavell connection

No. 132 seems to have been reserved for use as a hearse van when new, since its first and much publicised duty came on 15th May 1919 when it was used to convey the body of Nurse Edith Cavell from Dover to London, on repatriation. Executed by the Germans in 1915 for helping captured allied soldiers escape back to Britain, she was subsequently honoured as a war hero with a commemoration service held in Westminster Abbey before final interment in her home city of Norwich. For this reason many older railwaymen would refer to any utility van as a "Nurse Cavell van".

The procedure was repeated just two months later when van 132 was again used to bring the body of Captain

Charles Fryatt from Dover to London. Captain Fryatt had defied the orders of a German U-boat captain to stop and instead had attempted to ram the enemy with his own ship; the GER-owned SS *Brussels*. Fryatt and his ship were subsequently captured and he was tried and executed in a similar manner to Nurse Cavell. His repatriation and honour as a war hero followed on 8th July 1919, with a ceremony this time held in St Paul's Cathedral.

Van 132 may not have been released from special duties for a while yet, since its next recorded official duty was to convey the body of the Unknown Warrior back to London from Dover on 10th November 1920. After this the van appears to have been released to ordinary traffic, soon to be joined by its 44 similar production brethren. Once in Southern Railway ownership, the vans were gradually repainted into Maunsell green livery (which proved to be a protracted process; taking from 1925 until August 1930), with numbers 1972-91 being specifically reserved for boat train use and having roof board destination brackets added in 1930. SR Diagram 960 was allocated; marking out the SECR vans from all subsequent SR luggage van construction – although this distinction was possibly somewhat academic as only minor dimensional detail and internal differences separated them. With the coming of World War 2, all boat train traffic ceased and the boat-train-

Above - *An almost anonymous SECR van at Ramsgate in 1929. This does have the four destination slates and even at this early date, a good coating of grime. On the original print it is just possible to discern SECR lettering making this one of the Ashford 1922 batch that retained brown livery for longer than the earlier Bristol-built vans.*

J A G Coltas

Right - *A close-up of the axlebox on SECR utility van DS792 at Ashford in 1972. Apart from the initials "SR" cast into the cover, this fitting was identical for all 4-wheeled vans regardless of build date.*

Author

VARIATIONS ON LUGGAGE VANS

allocated vans might find themselves on any duty. Five vans – numbers 1996, 2001/2/4/5 were fitted with through air pipes for pull-push duties in August 1939 and these were the last survivors of the SECR vans in normal traffic. Van 2003 was scheduled to be converted but could not be found in time, so 1996 played substitute. These replaced a number of ex-LBSCR six-wheeled passenger brake "air control vans", mostly on South Eastern or Central section duties but van 2004 was allocated to the Bournemouth West-Ringwood-Brockenhurst service.

Apart from one 1939 transfer to departmental service (van 2009 to rail cleaning van 282s) and a couple of wartime losses/conversions for military use, general withdrawal of the pre-Grouping vans began in 1946, including the prototype. The five air control vans remained on their duties until late 1962, in marked contrast to most of the others. However, practically every one entered departmental service, but for vans 1976/94 this did not take place until ten years after the remainder. Just why these two should have survived in normal traffic for so much longer is unknown, but both then also entered departmental use – numbered in the Southern Region DS70XXX series. Both have passed into preservation, No. 1976 on the Mid Hants Railway, no. 1994 on the Bluebell.

The later history of prototype van 1972 is typical, becoming departmental no. 374s in 1946, then DS374 allocated to the Electrical Power Supply Section until 1967. It then became internal user 082757 and ended its BR days at Guildford in 1991, in olive green livery. Seemingly just another utility van, by good fortune it was purchased by the Kent and East Sussex Railway and delivered to Wittersham Road station during 1992. Only then was its historical significance realised and it was cosmetically restored to SECR livery soon after purchase. Ownership disputes then clouded the issue but in 2004 it was decided to apply for a Heritage Lottery grant for full restoration, which was completed in 2010. At the time of writing, the van is now on display at Bodiam station, complete with internal hearse fittings and contains a small exhibition about Nurse Cavell, Captain Fryatt and the Unknown Soldier. If you are visiting the line, the exhibition is well worth a stop at Bodiam station. A small booklet has also been produced by the railway giving details of the van, its hearse duties and a

history of those honoured, which may be purchased at the railway's bookshops.

Covcars and General Utility Vans, 1925-39

The Southern Railway inherited a fair stock of luggage vans of pre-Grouping origin – indeed the last batch of 20 to LSWR design was completed during 1923, whilst covered carriage trucks were a separate and specialised small group of vans. They were characterised by having end doors and (in most cases) a higher pitched roof profile allowing them to be used specifically to carry either horse-drawn/internal combustion road vehicles or theatrical scenery. In 1925 Maunsell presented the Rolling Stock Committee with a proposal to construct some vehicles described as general utility vans – to incorporate all the features of the SECR Lynes-designed luggage vans plus end doors – enabling all types of traffic to be accommodated with just one design; hence the description. The estimated cost was around £800 each. For this, Lynes had dusted off the original 1916 drawings but added three end doors – two side hung and a drop flap which, when opened, rested on the buffers, allowing a road vehicle to be driven in from an end-loading dock – a facility found at practically all SR stations. Otherwise there were some detail changes in side elevation. Below the windows four ventilation bonnets were added and the position of the vacuum cylinder was revised slightly. The lack of ventilator bonnets was always the easiest way to spot an ex-SECR example, as all later SR-built luggage vans had this feature as well. Twenty general utility vans were initially ordered – later revised to fifty.

However, there appeared no great hurry to construct them and before this took place a major reorganisation of Ashford, Brighton, Eastleigh and Lancing Works was mooted. This may have reduced the capacity for new construction for a while and perhaps for this reason the order was eventually placed with the Midland Railway Carriage and Wagon Company, who supplied all fifty at a cost of £659 each between March and May 1928. The estimated cost was marginally reduced by having reconditioned vacuum cylinders provided by the Southern – the work of fitting these taking place on delivery at Eastleigh Works. Running numbers were 2023-72 – in the "luggage van" series of the van list rather than as covered

Opposite top - Departmental van DS70031 at Axminster on 15th June 1961, painted green with black ends. Formerly SECR no. 153 and later SR No. 1994, this was completed at Ashford Works in August 1922, renumbered and repainted in SR livery in August 1930 (the last one to be done). It has "L" angle end stanchions, while the end windows were added on departmental conversion to an Engineer's mess and tool van in June 1959, allocated to Broad Clyst depot and it was "lost" to the Western Region in the boundary changes of January 1963. Apart from the five air control vans this was one of the other two ex-SECR vehicles to remain in ordinary service after 1948 and was purchased by the Bluebell Railway from Taunton as DW70031 in 1973.
A E West

Opposite bottom - M7 0-4-4T No. 30056 leaving Wimborne with the 2.08pm Brockenhurst-Bournemouth pull-push service on 7th September 1962. The loco is propelling a Maunsell pull-push set and one of the SECR "air control vans" over the River Stour bridge. The LMS full brake at the rear is not fitted so has to trail the locomotive. Some nifty shunting will be required at

Things are not always what they seem – particularly with departmental conversions! This is ex-SECR van DS1026 (ex-SECR 125/SR 1977) in what the photographer describes as bauxite but was probably gulf red livery (which faded to orange-brown) at Axminster on 31st May 1962. Converted to a mess van in October 1948, this has now been plywood sheeted entirely save for the doors so presents a similar appearance to the BR-built utility vans of 1951. Being based at Exeter it too, was "lost" to the Western Region in 1963 and also ended its days at Taunton permanent way depot. Southern Carriage & Wagon Society (SCWS) notes give the livery as grey originally, then black and finally gulf red, although it is believed it ended its days again in black as DW1026 about 1980.

A E West

carriage trucks – as if to emphasise their universal role and following on from luggage vans of SECR origin – as if to emphasise their parentage as well. Perhaps because of the later fitting of the vacuum cylinders the vans did not enter traffic in numerical order; nos 2024-30 being the first, 2023/36 the last. They were also actually labelled "General Utility Van" on the solebars – perhaps the only batch to be so, however photographs of the next few batches when new have not been found to prove this assertion right or wrong. In carriage working notices they were described as "Van U" - presumably an abbreviation for utility. Diagram 3101 was allocated and this gives the length over end doors as 32ft 4¼ in - 4¼ in longer than the pure luggage van version. However, the next couple of batches constructed were at first allocated Diagram 3102 and were noted as 32ft 6in long but whether this was over hinges rather than end planking is unclear. What is clear is that all were later recorded as Diagram 3101. Details of all these batches are as follows: -

2023 - 2072 Built Midland RCW Co March-May 1928
2251 - 2280 Built Ashford April-July 1929
2371 - 2410* Built Ashford April-July 1931
2411 - 2460* Built Ashford September 1931-February 1932
2241 - 2250 Built Ashford February-April 1933
2491 - 2500 Built Ashford February-April 1933

* These batches were initially allocated Diagram 3102.
Again, entry into traffic was often not in numerical order.

All were identical with even-planked sides and were as shown in general arrangement drawing E26385A, reproduced herewith, although this drawing was actually produced to show the revised lettering specification of 1936 with the letters XP (for express passenger) and the wheelbase of 21ft added in white characters. Van 2435, the subject of the drawing, was actually ex-works in January 1932 and was not lettered "General Utility Van" but instead carried the code word "COVCAR" in yellow (not gilt shaded black) in the lower right-hand corner of each side. Possibly this was the first batch to carry the revised branding. The construction of these brought the number of

Probably the most extensive departmental conversion of them all, this is generator van 97s rebuilt from SECR van 1987 in July 1946 to provide power for Bulleid sleeping/inspection saloon 100s. For this purpose it was re-bodied in Bulleid style to match the inspection saloon and repainted malachite green. Once 100s was scrapped the van was repainted grey and later became internal user 081033 in 1958, usually to be found around Eastleigh loco shed or works.

S C Nash

Covcars to 190 and production then ceased for five years. Some (perhaps all) of the 2251-80 batch had collapsible fruit shelving fitted from May 1929 to cater for this rather seasonal traffic – replacing a number of ancient pre-Grouping LSWR and SECR passenger coaches hitherto employed. Probably these fittings were not permanent in nature and could be removed and refitted as needed. Van 2266 was branded "For poultry traffic, Heathfield-London Bridge" in 1930, replacing a couple of ex-LBSCR covered goods vans on this working while van 2040 was roof boarded "Heathfield & District Poultry" in January 1933. Both were rare examples of a permanent allocation for a utility van.

The next batch – in fact the last Covcars built before British Railways days – appeared in November/December 1938. These were numbers 1731-80 and were the first to have 2+2 uneven planked sides (ie. alternate pairs of wide and narrow planks). Despite this feature, the side doors were even-planked and in this respect these vans were unique. This feature was faithfully reproduced on the 1963 Hornby Dublo (later Wrenn/Dapol) 4mm scale model – even if the running number and over scale hinge detail was wrong. The end doors remained the same as previously. Diagram 3101 was again allocated and the vans were a joint Ashford / Eastleigh production – the underframes at the former, the bodywork at the latter.

Most of the original 1928 and 1929 batches of Covcars remained in service until 1962/63 while the rest of the 1931-33 vehicles were taken out of ordinary traffic between 1965 and 1970 so none is likely to have received rail blue livery. Indeed, some of these vans were still in the crimson lake livery employed between 1949 and 1956 at withdrawal – not that this was always easy to see under the grime. After 1956 Southern Region green was applied,

replaced by rail blue from about 1966 onwards. Several entered departmental service and were modified to varying degrees in the process. This could range from quite minor alterations to a complete stripping of the bodywork for use as a crane runner. Ten became Fawley block oil train barrier wagons in 1965, repainted in freight stock fitted bauxite livery and renumbered as S69000-9, however their underframe construction was not up to withstanding the buffing shocks of a train of tankers and they distorted badly. All ten were withdrawn from these duties in October 1966. The 1938 uneven-planked batch fared rather better with some lasting until 1982. Relatively few of these entered departmental service but a number have passed into preservation.

Luggage Vans 1933-1939

Perhaps through a desire to save money, or perhaps because the end-doors on the Covcars were not being used as much as had been expected, a reversion to the luggage van design took place from 1933. By comparison, BR built very many four-wheeled and bogie covered carriage trucks (coded CCT) after nationalisation all equipped with end doors. Maybe this was symptomatic of the era as in the 1930s carriage of horse-drawn road vehicles had practically ceased but the equivalent traffic in road motor vehicles had yet to build up. Whatever the reasons, once construction of luggage vans recommenced this continued until 1951, making these easily the most numerous variant of utility van. The BR mainland code for these was PMV (parcels and miscellaneous van), PLV (passenger luggage van) on the Isle of Wight.

These reverted to the ex-SECR design, but with the addition of side ventilator bonnets and the same alterations to the vacuum cylinder position as used on the Covcars of

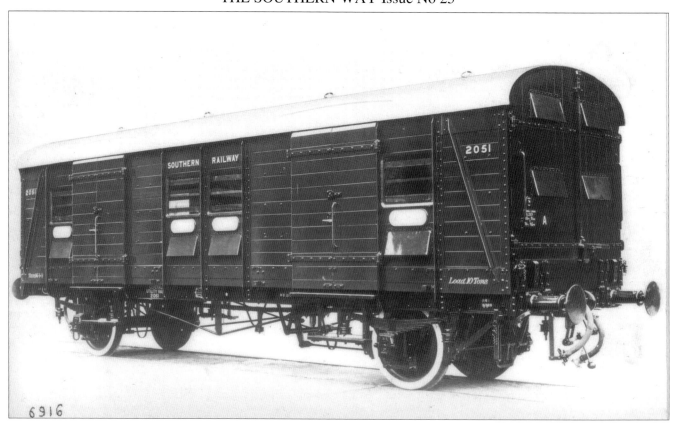

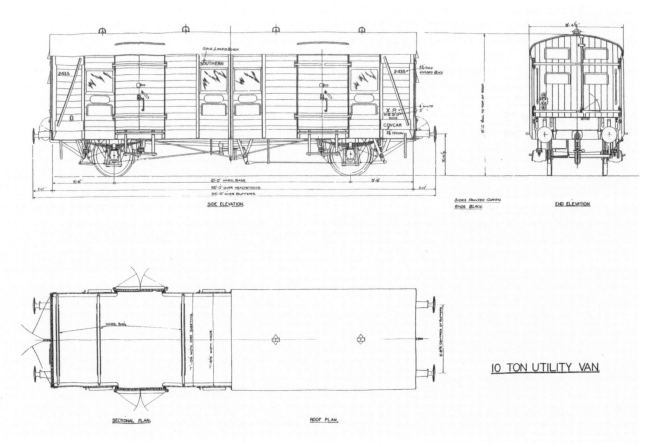

10 TON UTILITY VAN

SIDE ELEVATION.

END ELEVATION.

SECTIONAL PLAN.

ROOF PLAN.

Opposite top - Covcar 2051 officially recorded by the Southern Railway in April 1928 at Eastleigh Works (the date of construction by Midland RCW Co. of 3/3/28 and works location 15 for Eastleigh are painted on the solebar below the "Load 10 Tons" inscription) – after the reconditioned vacuum cylinder had been fitted. The van entered traffic on 12th April 1928. Note the "General Utility Van" title on the solebar and the absence at this stage of the code word Covcar. The livery is Maunsell green sides, black ends and underframe with a white roof. The end doors are obvious, as is the letter A on the van end, indicating that Ashford Works would be responsible for maintenance. This van ran until December 1962 and became departmental DS70220 exactly two years later.   *SR Official*

Opposite bottom - General arrangement drawing E26385A, showing the original Covcar design, allocated SR Diagram 3101. This drawing had been amended since January 1936 to show revised lettering details, including the omission of the word "Railway" and the addition of the XP and WB 21'-0" brandings in white. The Covcar code is also shown in 3¼ inch yellow letters whilst the word "Southern" is in gold, lined black; the numerals are also 3¾ inches high gold but shaded black. These last livery details therefore appear to relate to early Bulleid changes of 1938.

This page - Covcar 2435 - interestingly the same van as depicted in the general arrangement drawing herewith – as outshopped in August 1935 but with the lettering Covcar instead of the General Utility Van title. New in January 1932, it ran until January 1967. Note the change in style of door grab handles – shorter than previously.   *SR Official*

Opposite top - *A broadside official view in November 1938 of Covcar 1737, showing the 2+2 planked sides but even-planked doors. These were also outshopped with grey instead of white roofs. In common with most of this batch, the van remained in traffic until 1982. Towards the end of their lives some CCT's had their end doors plated over at the bottom so that they would not open and so were effectively considered as PMV's. By this time TOPS codes had replaced the former descriptions – these being NOV for the Covcars and NQV for the luggage vans.* SR Official

Opposite bottom - *Covcar 2372 – one of those originally recorded as Diagram 3102 - at Eastleigh on 29th October 1949. This is still in Southern Railway green livery with black ends but has the number prefixed by a small 's' in place of the company title. Note the letters CCT have been added in the lower right-hand corner of the side. Built in June 1931, the van was withdrawn in January 1966 and became departmental tool van DS70240 in March 1966, finally being sold to the Isle of Wight Steam Railway, probably for its underframe to be re-used under one of their preserved carriage bodies.* A E West

This page - *Departmental CCT van DS70207, formerly no. 2040 built by Midland RCW Co in 1928. This was a Motive Power tool van based at Fratton and was finished in bright red livery and is coupled to former LSWR "Ironclad" coach DS232. Withdrawn in December 1962, it assumed its departmental role exactly a year later and apart from the overhead live wire flashes appears to have undergone no external modifications. It was this van that was roof boarded "Heathfield and District Poultry" in January 1933.* T A Barry Collection

1928. In side elevation they were therefore almost indistinguishable from them. The first batch of 50, numbers 2181-2230 appeared from Ashford Works between October 1934 and March 1935. Diagram 3103 was allocated. Further batches were constructed up to 1939, bringing the total to 445 examples, as follows: -

1054 - 1153 Built Ashford November 1936-April 1937
1154 - 1250 Built Ashford April 1935-February 1936
1921 - 1970 Built Ashford October-December 1938
1251 - 1358 Built Ashford February-October 1939
All the above had even-planked sides and ends.

In 1939 the uneven-planking made its appearance and forty were completed in this style; numbers being 1359-1398, out -shopped from Ashford between July and December 1939. These were not actually a separate order, merely a continuation of the previous and some even-planked vans actually entered traffic after the first uneven-planked example (which was no 1359, in July 1939).

Carriage working notices now seldom stipulated that a Covcar was to be provided for any particular service and either type of van (including those of SECR origin) could be used indiscriminately. Those without end doors were simply labelled Luggage in place of Covcar. Few specific allocation brandings have been noted for these batches – certainly not before British Railways ownership: however van 1201 was transferred to departmental service as 281s between June 1939 and January 1947, after which it retook its former traffic department number. This is described in the service stock register as a rail-cleaning van allocated to the electrical engineer in the same manner as ex -SECR van 2009 noted earlier. Presumably both were used to clear the electrified third rail of ice during the winter months and they were replaced on such duties by a far greater number of ex-LBSCR trailer cars similarly converted from 1946 onwards. Van 1215 was labelled "For Dover Ferry Service", possibly as soon as the Night Ferry began to operate in October 1936. This van, and No 1318, were recorded as having French-type steam heating couplers fitted between 1948 and 1954 so perhaps ran further into France than Dunkirk during that period. They also had chaining down rings attached to the solebars in the same manner as ferry brake vans 1-3, to be described in part 3 of these articles.

A number of luggage vans from these batches were converted into mobile workshops for the War Department from 1940 onwards. The first two (formerly luggage vans 1086 and 1200) accompanied the British Expeditionary Force to France and were soon in German hands but a further 21 conversions followed between then and 1944. These took vans 1056/73, 1112/27/65/88/95/96, 1230/39/51, 1300/12/37, 1948, 2190/92/98, 2211/21 and SECR van 2008 out of SR ownership and none were ever returned. Most of the early ones went to the Middle East in 1941/2 while the others served at home or in Europe following the D-Day landings. Some may have returned to this country later as several ended their days at such Army locations as Long Marston and Longmoor in the 1960s. Most of the units comprised a luggage van converted to a workshop and either two or three standard SR covered goods wagons, which provided a store, office, welding and/or generator facility. A few others received wartime damage and at least two even -planked vans (nos. 1106 and 1191) were replanked in the 2+2 style. Some others were noted in traffic during the war years painted grey instead of green - almost certainly due to a shortage of paint but lettered otherwise in orthodox style. In a later article the livery aspects will be dealt with in greater detail.

Practically all the rest from the 1934 and 1935 batches entered departmental service between 1950 and 1962, many becoming Signal and Telegraph tool vans. For this purpose they often had a window cut into the centre of each end, below the ventilator hood as well as repainting into whatever departmental livery was then in vogue – red, green, grey or black being the most common. Some of these have since passed into preservation from the 1970s onwards. Van 2226 was an early grounding as a store at Brockenhurst down goods yard in 1963 – one of the first to be so used. A few of the 1936-39 vehicles became departmental stock from about 1963 onwards but many more of these remained in general service until as late as 1983. Fourteen were allocated to South Eastern division bicycle traffic from 1950 onwards and received a white bicycle stencil on each side to denote this. Most came from the pre-war batches but at least three were later vehicles with 2+2 planking. Nine others were equipped with tethering gear for "BRUTE"s – British Railways Universal Trolley Equipment – those bright blue mesh parcels trolleys that could be seen at most large stations during the 1960s and 1970s. These included

Opposite top - Unfortunately from a rather scratched negative, this is luggage van 1171 at Waterloo when fairly new in 1936 showing Southern Railway livery and lettering, including the branding "Luggage" in yellow. Built in August 1935, this van became Signal and Telegraph tool van DS29 in February 1955, allocated to Exeter. Yet another vehicle "lost " to the Western Region in 1963, it was finally withdrawn around 1975.   *HMRS Collection*

Opposite bottom - A September 1935 vintage van, S1235, carrying early British Railways minimal lettering and crimson lake livery, in a long line of similar vans, probably around 1950. The number is in the left-hand corner (this was soon revised to the RH end and another S suffix added) while the code PMV appears in small letters just above the hand brake lever. Yet another departmental transfer, this became DS13 in February 1954 allocated to Selhurst depot.

Author's Collection

numbers 1064, 1289, 1318/36/88/95 as well as three from post-1939 batches. No external modifications are known but they were lettered appropriately to indicate the internal arrangements and were confined to Central and South Eastern division circuit workings. British Rail ceased its parcels collection and delivery service in 1981 and this meant a rapid demise for luggage vans of all descriptions and large numbers of utility vans were condemned soon after – many at locations well away from the Southern Region. Some of these passed into departmental or internal

use, again not necessarily at SR locations while others have been purchased for preservation – either direct from traffic or after a period in service use.

This brings the story of the four-wheeled Covcars and luggage van development to 1939 so would be a good place to stop. The next article will continue the design development of these vehicles until production ceased in 1955 and will then look at the gangwayed bogie luggage vans built on old LSWR underframes in 1930/31 plus the scenery vans.

This page - Uneven-planked van S1370S at Clapham Junction around 1963, in Southern Region green and carrying the more informative lettering of the period. Built in October 1939 this lasted until July 1980, then becoming internal user 041503, somewhere on the Eastern Region.
                                                                                                    T A Barry Collection

Opposite top - Chipman's weed killing train at Cuffley (Herts) in the spring of 1955. Two SR utility vans provide the riding and control accommodation; numbered CWT1/2 and would appear to be formerly numbers 2201/3 from the 1934/5 original batch of luggage vans. Both of these were withdrawn in October 1954 and were not converted for railway departmental service. The vans (and tanks) are almost certainly painted mid- green with white lettering, which was Chipman's usual livery. The company was based at Horsham and held a contract with BR for weed killing for very many years – these vans being at least the second incarnation of their train. The roof boards on CWT1 read "Chipman Chemical Company Limited", those on CWT 2 read "Atlantacide Weed Killer Train". The locomotive is an ex-GNR J6 0-6-0. *BR Official*

Opposite bottom - Signal and telegraph staff van DS4, allocated to Hither Green is seen at Stewarts Lane, possibly in the early 1960s. Formerly traffic van 1189, this dates from June 1935 and was converted for S & T use in November 1953, when the end windows were provided. The livery might be black, grey, green or red but according to the Southern Carriage and Wagon Society (SCWS) notes it was originally painted red, later black. It was last noted in 1989.
                                                                                                    The Lens of Sutton Association

Almost anonymous luggage van 1271 at Eastleigh on 29th July 1950 – probably green under all that grime! Indeed, the author as a youngster thought there were three classes of utility van – red ones - mistakenly of LMS origin, green ones of SR origin and brown ones (which were by far the majority), which he considered as goods stock. It was many years before the full story emerged and that they were all SR passenger van stock, whatever the apparent colour. However some vans were actually constructed at Wolverton Works during 1951 so perhaps the LMS idea wasn't quite so fanciful after all!! Van 1271 dates from May 1939 and was one of the last survivors of the even-planked variety, running until March 1981.
A E West

SOUTHERN EPHEMERA

A FURTHER SELECTION OF WONDERFUL SOUTHERN (AND CONSTITUENT) PAPERWORK COURTESY OF MICHAEL BROOKS.

London and South Western Railway.

1892 HOSPITAL PASS
THIRD CLASS

Any person found using this Pass who is not entitled to such user will be liable to prosecution.

PASS ONE PERSON (COMPANY'S SERVANT, WIFE or dependent CHILD)

Between _Eastleigh_ _Southampton_

and _Winchester_

Date _26th April_ to _30th June_ 1918

Issued by _____   H. A. WALKER, General Manager.

SUBJECT TO CONDITIONS ON OTHER SIDE.

TRAVEL DE LUXE.

South Eastern & Chatham Railway

The "THANET" PULLMAN LIMITED
To Margate, Broadstairs & Ramsgate

EVERY SUNDAY during the Winter Season, 1921-22.

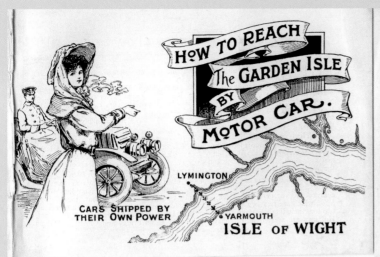

HOW TO REACH
The GARDEN ISLE
BY
MOTOR CAR.

CARS SHIPPED BY THEIR OWN POWER

LYMINGTON
YARMOUTH
ISLE OF WIGHT

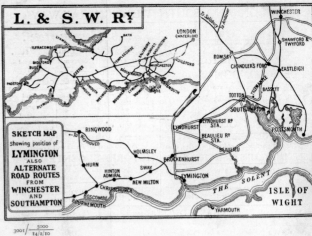

L. & S.W. Ry.

SKETCH MAP showing position of LYMINGTON ALSO ALTERNATE ROAD ROUTES FROM WINCHESTER AND SOUTHAMPTON

THE SOLENT
ISLE OF WIGHT

Loading Motor Cars at Lymington.

MOTORING IN THE ISLE OF WIGHT.

NO Motor Tour through England can be considered complete which does not include a run round the Isle of Wight (sixty miles) The most convenient point for crossing is at Lymington, on the South side of the charming New Forest, where the London and South Western Railway Company has provided efficient accommodation for such traffic, including slipways whereby cars can be shipped by their own power on to specially constructed boats, thus entirely obviating the necessity of lifting, and removing a difficulty which hitherto has deterred many from visiting the lovely "Garden Isle."

The boats—towed by fast, powerful tugs—quickly negotiate the passage, which is the shortest and most sheltered, to the Island. On week-days the boats leave Lymington Town Station Wharf at 9*30, 11 30 a.m., 2.30 and 4*45 p.m. for Yarmouth, and Yarmouth at 8.0 a.m., 12.30 and 5*30 p.m. for Lymington. Cars should be upon the Wharf half-an-hour before these times. (*March to September only

Special passages can be arranged at other times during the day upon previous notice being given to the Stationmaster, Lymington (Telephone No. 7), the extra charge being 10s. per car on week-days and £1 per car on Sundays above the ordinary rates, which are 10s. for cars not exceeding half-a-ton, and 15s. for cars not exceeding two tons including wharfage and porterage at Lymington and Yarmouth. N B.—Bank Holidays are treated as ordinary week-days, Good Friday and Christmas Day as Sundays.

Loading Motor Cars at Lymington.
Cars already in Boat with others waiting to be loaded.

The L. & S.W R. Tug "Carrier" towing two Boats loaded with Motor Cars from Lymington to Yarmouth.

Unloading Motor Cars at Yarmouth, I. of W.

KING ARTHUR

"KING ARTHUR"

FEW people—even those who use the Continental Boat Trains frequently—realise the difficult route over which they travel. The distance from Victoria to Dover Marine Station, 77½ miles, is not great, and the time taken, 95 to 100 minutes, does not seem outstanding. Since no Railway management wants to keep its trains one second longer on a particular run than is necessary, with the cost of transportation where it is to-day, it goes without saying that there are reasons why a faster run is not accomplished.

Chief among these is the fact that the Main Line from Victoria to Dover is the steepest of any Main Line out of London. The North and South Downs, which cut across the route in many places, cause it to resemble a series of switch-backs, containing gradients which require harder Express locomotive work than is to be found in most parts of this country. A second factor that has made difficult the operation of an intensive Continental Boat Train Service has been that hitherto it has not been possible to employ locomotives of the heaviest class on these trains. For the past two years, however, the Engineers of the Southern Railway have been hard at work re-building and strengthening the various bridges on the route, in order that now, in the Summer of 1925, the Boat Trains may be hauled in most cases by locomotives of the "King Arthur" Class, which are the most powerful on the whole of the Southern system, and among the biggest in the country.

The public conception of the use of a larger locomotive is that it will cover a given distance in a shorter time. And, of course, so it will. But there is a much more economical—and efficient—method of employing the heavier locomotives, and that is to maintain the present exacting schedules with a considerably increased load. The public benefits directly by this method in that more passengers can be carried by the fast trains down or up, and the possibility of crowding during Holiday rushes is lessened. The present Boat Trains, when hauled by "King Arthur" engines, now weigh approximately 425 tons, and an interesting comparison is thus afforded with 1864, the year in which the old London, Chatham and Dover Railway first ran Boat Train Specials. These trains weighed 125 tons, and took 20 minutes longer to do the journey than to-day.

Leaving Victoria Station the driver immediately faces a heavy gradient of 1 in 64 leading up to Grosvenor Road Bridge over the Thames. Some distance afterwards the line becomes a long upward pull, mostly at 1 in 120, to Knockholt Tunnel where the summit is reached. Thence there is a steep descent through Sevenoaks to Tonbridge, where a speed restriction is enforced over the bend which leads to the junction points. From Tonbridge to Ashford the only really straight portion of the line is encountered, and along this 26¼ miles the Boat Trains are "booked" at approximately 60 miles per hour.

At Ashford the Continental Express enters on the last stage of its run, consisting of 21 miles of undulating track. Soon Folkestone Central is reached and passed, almost immediately followed by Folkestone Junction from which the Harbour Branch deviates on the right-hand side. For Dover Marine the driver continues straight ahead, and for a few miles you traverse one of the most remarkable pieces of track in this country, with the English Channel only a few yards away on the one side, and the white cliffs of Kent towering above the train on the other.

And now the driver slowly takes the curve into the new Marine Station at Dover. You catch a glimpse of the old town before your carriage comes to rest, and in a relatively short space of time you feel the Channel breeze on your face as the steamer points its bows for France.

* * * * * * * *

A word about the journey in the reverse direction. You may have noticed sometimes that your train does not follow the same route. A glance at the map in this folder will show you that at Ashford there is a fork, the line to the right leading through Maidstone East, Otford and Swanley Junction, joining the Main Line again at Bickley Junction. This alternative route is brought into use if the arrival of your boat at Dover or Folkestone has been delayed by some cause or other earlier in the journey. A lengthy Customs examination or an abnormal amount of baggage may also delay the departure of the Boat Train, in which case the Maidstone route may be used. The gradients between Ashford and Swanley are severe, and a slightly longer schedule time is allowed.

On the Main Line, the steepest gradient is met between Tonbridge and Sevenoaks, and it involves exceedingly hard locomotive work with a heavy train weighing four hundred tons or over. As the crowded Suburban area is entered the task of sandwiching your Boat Train successfully among the many local trains occupying the track at the same time becomes more intricate.

Whichever way you are journeying, from London or towards it, you may be sure that there are few Main Line routes in this country which present such a difficult task to a traffic department, on account of the heavy Suburban traffic, and of the gradients and curves with which the drivers have to contend; equally, there are few routes with more interesting historical associations, for these were the tracks over which thousands of British soldiers passed on their way to the War. Your way lies through a country-side as endeared to Englishmen who know it well as it is admired by those who see it for the first time through the windows of the Continental Express.

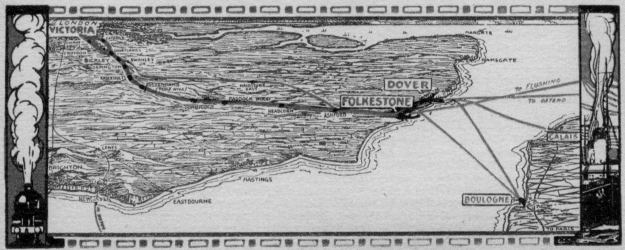

P.D.—6085—7/25—50.

Printed by McCORQUODALE & Co. LTD., London.

SOUTHERN
MIXED TRAFFIC LOCOMOTIVES
"Battle of Britain" Class

These new engines of the Southern Railway will bear names of personalities, aircraft, R.A.F stations and squadrons associated with the Battle of Britain, which was fought, for the most part, over territory served by the Southern Railway.

This new class of "Pacific" engines, for fast passenger and express freight trains, is similar in design to the well known "Merchant Navy" and "West Country" engines. They are being built in the Brighton Works of the Southern Railway, to the design of Mr. O. V. Bulleid, Chief Mechanical Engineer

Headquarters .
Waterloo Station]

[Sir Eustace Missenden, *General Manager*.

NEW ENGINES FOR THE SOUTHERN RAILWAY

Forty engines of the new "Battle of Britain" Class are now being built by the Southern Railway. Of modern design, many features are included which have proved so successful in the "Merchant Navy" and "West Country" Class engines.

The new locomotives bear names of personalities, aircraft, R.A.F. stations and squadrons associated with the Battle of Britain. Air-smoothed and capable of drawing freight as well as passenger trains at high speed, they can be used on any of the main lines of the Southern Railway.

Engines and tenders will bear the Southern Railway pre-war livery of green and yellow and each one will carry a name, with coat of arms or badge, on the sides of the air smoothed casing.

The first of these engines, No. 21C151 is named "Winston Churchill," and the names of others to complete the series are as follows :—

Lord Dowding	Fighter Command
Sir Keith Park	Fighter Pilot
Lord Beaverbrook	
Hurricane	Spitfire

R.A.F STATIONS

Tangmere	Croydon
Kenley	Manston
Hawkinge	Biggin Hill

R.A.F SQUADRONS

17	46	92	2 9	253	602
23	66	141	222	257	603
25	73	145	229	264	605
41	74	2 3	249	501	615

and two further squadrons

AD 5642 $\frac{500}{2947}$ Printed by McCorquodale & Co. Ltd., London—48633.

LONDON BRIGHTON AND SOUTH COAST RAILWAY

NOTICE.

Pullman Car Trains.

Commencing on Friday, 1st December, the following **PULLMAN EXPRESS TRAINS** between **VICTORIA AND BRIGHTON** will have First Class Carriages attached—

The 10.0 a.m. and 3.50 p.m. DOWN TRAINS
FROM
VICTORIA TO BRIGHTON.

The 1.20 p.m. and 5.45 p.m. UP TRAINS
FROM
BRIGHTON TO VICTORIA.

(By Order) J. P. KNIGHT,
General Manager

LONDON BRIDGE TERMINUS.
29th November, 1882.

Printed by LETTS, SON CO., LIMITED, London, E.C

London and South Western Railway.

GENERAL MANAGER'S OFFICE,
WATERLOO STATION,
LONDON, S.E.

21st August, 1914.

NOTICE TO STAFF.

VOLUNTEERS OR MEN ENLISTING FOR SERVICE DURING THE PERIOD OF THE WAR.

Members of the Staff who have been given permission to offer their services to the Government during the present crisis and have been accepted will be considered as on leave without pay whilst absent from this cause, and their contributions to the Superannuation Fund or Auxiliary Pension Funds, the deductions in respect of which are made through the paybill, will, until they return or definitely leave the service, be borne by the Company upon the understanding that in the case of any of the men deciding to leave the service they shall have no claim to the return of the contributions paid by the Company during their absence.

H. A. WALKER,
General Manager,

NOTICE TO STAFF.

It has been decided that the Wives and Families and other Dependants of this Company's Men who are called up for service with the Regulars or Territorials or of Men who volunteer for service in the Army during the period of the war shall be given such an allowance by the Company as will, with Government pay, be sufficient for their maintenance during the time the Bread-winners are away from home. The same arrangement will be made for Wives and Families or Dependants of men who are called up to serve as Naval Reservists or Volunteers.

It has also been decided that positions in the service shall be found for the men on their return, and that the Salary or Wage will then be paid according to the scale to which they would have been entitled had they not joined the Colours

Contributions to Superannuation and Auxiliary Pension Funds will be paid by the Railway Company.

LONDON, S.E., 31*st December*, 1914.

TO THE STAFF

EXTRACT FROM DAILY PAPER :—

"If we were asked to quote an example of strenuous
"and sustained patriotism, we should point to the working
"staff, say of the London & South Western Railway
"or any other of the great industrial concerns specially
"connected with war preparations. They work night
"and day with the same patriotic devotion as the
"sailors of the Fleet and the soldiers of the Army."

I desire to convey to the whole of the employees of the Company my appreciation of the loyal and patriotic manner in which they have carried out the onerous duties they have been called upon to perform since the outbreak of War.

The requirements of the Admiralty and War Office in addition to the ordinary business of the Company, have necessitated long hours of work, and in some cases continuous night and day duty, and it is gratifying to be able to record that such services have been loyally and ungrudgingly performed.

Unfortunately the end of our labours in connection with the War is not yet in sight, but I feel sure that I can continue to rely upon the same devotion to duty in the future as in the past.

With all good wishes for the New Year.

CHRISTMAS 1940

THE SOUTHERN RAILWAY

request the pleasure of the Company of

Mr. Sheriff W. L. Threlford

on the occasion of the

OFFICIAL OPENING OF THE ELECTRIFIED LINE
TO BRIGHTON AND WORTHING BY THE
LORD MAYOR OF LONDON

on Friday, 30th December, 1932.

ON RECEIPT OF YOUR ACCEPTANCE THE NECESSARY TICKETS WILL BE
FORWARDED TOGETHER WITH INVITATION TO THE OFFICIAL LUNCHEON
TO BE GIVEN BY THE MAYOR AND CORPORATION OF BRIGHTON

R.S.V.P. to
GENERAL MANAGER'S OFFICE,
SOUTHERN RAILWAY
WATERLOO STATION, S.E.1   PROGRAMME ON BACK

PROGRAMME

INAUGURAL TRIP TO BRIGHTON AND WORTHING,
30th December, 1932.

VICTORIA (Platform No. 15)	dep. 11 12 a.m.
WORTHING	arr. 12.26 p.m.

Reception by His Worship The Mayor of Worthing.

WORTHING	dep. 12.45 p.m.
BRIGHTON	arr. 1 5 p.m.

Reception by His Worship The Mayor of Brighton.
Lunch at the Royal Pavilion by invitation of the Mayor and Corporation   1 15 p.m.

BRIGHTON	dep. 3.20 p.m.
VICTORIA	arr. 4.20 p.m.

SOUTHERN RAILWAY

GENERAL MANAGER'S OFFICE

MESSAGE TO THE STAFF

To all my Southern Railway Colleagues,

The exchange of messages of good cheer and goodwill as between one another at this Christmastide of 1940 has a deeper meaning for us all.

Most of us have had many anxieties and difficulties to contend with, and in sending a personal message to each one of you I want to tell you how much I and my brother Officers of the Company admire and appreciate the dogged, steadfast way in which the work of the Southern Railway has been carried on during the past year in face of unprecedented conditions.

1940 will never be forgotten by those of us of the Southern Railway who have lived and served through it ; of that I feel sure. The collapse of France ; the evacuation of the B.E.F. from Dunkerque ; the subsequent strain which was thrown on to us, and the way in which it was surmounted—these things will remain in our memories always. The handling of the traffic of the returning Armies was a feat which aroused the admiration of the whole Nation, and we may all be proud to have had a hand in it. Then came the very real threat of invasion, and with it the extraordinary precautions, so greatly affecting this railway, which were taken in face of the gathering German armies on the other side of the Channel. Finally the Blitzkrieg, starting on our Kent and Sussex Coasts, then creeping inland, culminating in the early days of September, in its full blast of destruction and attempted intimidation.

We can say without any fear of contradiction that never in the history of railways have railwaymen and women of every rank, grade and classification, from the top to the bottom, had to carry on their work under such conditions. Much depended (and still does depend) on the men and women of the Southern Railway, continuously refusing to be intimidated, but instead carrying on their difficult duty undismayed in the face of the worst that Hitler and his Nazis can do.

The Minister of Transport, Lieut.-Colonel J. T. C. Moore-Brabazon, in a recent speech said : " The second battle of Waterloo concerned not armies but railways, and the Southern Railway had achieved as big a victory as ever had been seen."

We have all learnt many things in the course of the last few months : different ways of doing things, willingness to accept responsibility suddenly thrust on unaccustomed shoulders ; grievous strain, long hours and even personal sorrows have had to be borne. Borne they have been, and most cheerfully, and in sending you once more my Best Wishes for CHRISTMAS and throughout the NEW YEAR I do so with every sincerity, because I know how splendidly it has been earned.

The holiday this year will be short and sweet : so be it. British railwaymen and women, no less than the British Public whom they serve, have proved that " they can take it." Now we are rejoicing in the knowledge that our boys, both here and overseas, and in all the Fighting Services can " give it " too. So with renewed strength we shall continue our task on the Southern Railway until Hitler and his legions are no more.

May good fortune attend you, and God bless you all.

Eustace Missenden

WATERLOO STATION, LONDON.
December, 1940.

LAST CALL FOR THE BELLE

Jeffery Grayer recalls the end of regular steam working on the Bournemouth Belle in December 1966 together with the final week of its operation which saw a mixture of steam and diesel power in July 1967.

The end of December 1966 saw the last scheduled steam workings of the prestigious **_"Bournemouth Belle"_** Pullman train from London to Southampton and Bournemouth. Inaugurated on 5th July 1931 by the Southern Railway it did not operate during the period of the Second World War but was reintroduced on 7th October 1946. It finished almost exactly 36 years later to the day after its inauguration, on 9th July 1967. At first the train ran on summer Sundays but was extended to all summer weekdays and weekends finally becoming a daily service in 1936. Lord Nelson power pre-war gave way to Merchant Navy power from 1947 onwards although from time to time other motive power was substituted.

Merchant Navy Class No. 21C18 'British India

Line'' was at the helm of the first post-war service, departing Waterloo at 12:30 pm and arriving at Bournemouth Central in 2 hours 5 minutes. The return working from Bournemouth Central to Waterloo was scheduled to be five minutes quicker than the outward trip, leaving the former at 7.25 pm and arriving at the latter at 9:25 pm. This initial ''flirt'' with the new Pacific engines was interrupted by the advent of a trio of then new 1CO-CO1 diesel-electric locomotives. Also Bulleid products, Nos. 10201 to 10203 were completed jointly by Ashford and Brighton works between 1949 and 1954. These prototypes, alongside similar machines produced by Ivatt for the London Midland Region (Nos. 10000 and 10001), were frequently on the roster for the ''Bournemouth Belle'' and

35008 "Orient Line" waits departure at Waterloo with the down Belle in June 1966. As usual in the latter years no headboard was carried on this occasion. (Rail Photoprints)

Merchant Navy" Class 4-6-2 No. 35023 "Holland - Afrika Line" leaving Southampton Central station with the down 'Bournemouth Belle' from Waterloo. Note the dockyard cranes in the background, the large funnels visible on the left belong to RMS "Queen Elizabeth" then still in service. Tuesday 27th October 1964. (Geoff Plumb Collection)

non-Pullman ''Atlantic Coast Express'' workings. By July 1955, all these diesels had left for a new permanent home on the Midland Region, and the ''Bournemouth Belle'' once again became an all-steam affair behind Bulleid pacific engines.

The summer timetable of 1966 saw diesel traction replace scheduled steam workings on Sundays. The SR's native D6500 series diesels were drafted in, but to keep time, double-heading was required and failures were not uncommon. Bulleid pacifics frequently stood in for the booked diesels when this occurred. We take up the story in December 1966 when regular steam haulage was scheduled to come to an end being replaced by Brush Type 4 haulage. A number of these diesel locomotives, D1921 – D1926, had been loaned from the Western Region, the first arriving in September 1966, and were based at Eastleigh for the inter-regional services to Oxford, Banbury and beyond and to assist the ailing Bulleid Pacifics on the Bournemouth route. These Brush Type 4s had to stand in for the electro-diesel locomotives, E6000s, whose conversion from electric locomotives was proving particularly trying and lengthy. These Brush units represented a diesel breed which was not numerous on SR metals and in the type's formative years, reliability was poor.

Steam did not acquit itself particularly well during the last week of December 1966 as maintenance standards were by then pretty low, witness 34077 *602 Squadron* arriving at Southampton 45 minutes down, having run short

of steam west of Woking. After two halts for a "blow up" it limped into Farnborough where Crompton D6549 was coupled ahead of it to assist for the remainder of the journey.

Steam did come to the rescue on numerous occasions in 1967 when diesel failures or non availability of Type 4 locomotives occurred, instances being on 17th. February with 35013 *Blue Funnel,* 24th February with 34006 "Bude", 28th February with 35008 "Orient Line", 10th March with 34098 *Templecombe,* 11th March with 35007 *Aberdeen Commonwealth,* 12th March with 35028 *Clan Line* and again on 30th March and on April 14th when 34090 *Sir Eustace Missenden Southern Railway* deputised on the down Belle. Recourse was even had to Standard Class 5 73043 which was observed making heavy weather of the Pullman train, which could at times top 500 tons, near West Byfleet on 8th. May.

During the final week steam appeared on the Belle on two separate occasions when 34025 *Whimple* handled both down and up services on 3rd July and 34024 *Tamar Valley* had charge of the down train on 5th July whilst 34036 *Westward Ho* powered the up train on the same day. Brush Type 4s noted on the train in the final week included D1903/1924/1925/1926.Expectations were running high that the last day of operation of the Belle, 9th July, would see steam at its head. As a consequence of this many enthusiasts bought supplementary tickets (6/- (30p) from Bournemouth, 4/- (20p) from Southampton 2nd Class) and packed the

Last Call for the Belle

80869	BR Mk 1 Full Brake
Car No. 75 Third Class	Parlour Car
Car No. 61 Third Class	Kitchen Car
Car No. 64 Third Class	Parlour Car
Ursula	First Class Parlour Car
Phyllis	First Class Kitchen Car
Lucille	First Class Parlour Car
Aquila	First Class Kitchen Car
Car No. 76 Third Class	Parlour Car
Car No. 34	Second Class Parlour Car
E80631	BR Mk 1 Full Brake

lineside but in the end their hopes were dashed. Apparently senior management were taking a final trip on the service and had deemed that it should be diesel–operated at all costs such that if a diesel was not available then the train should be cancelled. No doubt steam did not fit the image of a modern railway on the brink of providing a new level of service with the coming electrification. In spite of the best efforts of the Wimbledon Diagram Office who had spoken to Nine Elms depot who had responded by cleaning 35023 *Holland Afrika Line*, rostering a senior driver for the task and looking out the old headboard which had not been seen on the train for some time, all these preparations behind the scenes were to no avail and a rather grimy D1924 was seen at the head of both services on the last day, with nine Pullman cars and two luggage vans, much to the chagrin of the waiting crowds and intending passengers. Indeed many of the supplementary tickets were not used as enthusiasts preferred to opt for the certainty of what was to be the final steam hauled up train in the shape of 35030 *Elder Dempster Lines* which was at the head of the 14:07 from Weymouth to Waterloo which pleasingly arrived 10 minutes early into the London terminus. The composition of the final Belle was as shown above.

Withdrawal of the Belle did not mean an end to the sight of Pullman cars in Clapham yard for, since the start of the new timetable, stock of the "Golden Arrow" was berthed and serviced overnight at the carriage shed at Clapham. The Railway Observer for November 1967 reported that sidings at Walton on Thames presented a sad sight being occupied by rakes of the former Bournemouth Belle Pullman cars, although not the standard brakes, not as yet marked "Condemned". By 14th. April 1968 several of the coaches were noted lying at Micheldever sidings marked as condemned i.e. Car No. 34, 61 and 74 together with

"Lucille", "Phyllis" and "Ursula". However, some made it into preservation including "Ursula" and Car No. 75 which are preserved at the 'Spot Gate' pub at Hilderstone by Ind Coope (Allied Breweries) and "Lucille" now owned by VSOE for use in their British Pullman train. Only the all electric Brighton Belle would carry on the tradition of Belles on the SR until this too finished in April 1972. However this was not quite the end of the Bournemouth Belle for a notable series of workings took place during 1986 sponsored by VSOE. On summer Saturdays in that year, the "Bournemouth Belle" recommenced from Waterloo, making use of authentic Pullman vehicles, albeit hauled by diesel traction in the form of a Class 33.

Pullman Cars

First and Second Class seats can be reserved on Pullman trains. The bookings are limited and a supplementary charge is payable. Supplementary tickets can be obtained at the starting station ticket office by personal or postal application, or from the Conductor on the train. Meals and light refreshments are served at all seats.

Bournemouth Belle

	Weekdays	Sundays
London Waterloo to Bournemouth Central	12 30	12 30
Bournemouth Central to London Waterloo	16 37	16 37
Southampton Central to London Waterloo	17 15	17 15

Pullman Car Supplementary Fees

	1st Class	2nd Class
Between London Waterloo and Southampton Central	6s. 6d.	4s. 0d.
Between London Waterloo and Bournemouth Central	8s. 0d.	6s. 0d.

1966/67 timetable extract detailing times of services and supplementary fares applicable to the Bournemouth Belle.

Above - Brush Type 4 D1924 heads the down Belle near Clapham Junction on 2nd July 1967, just one week before the last services ran. What of D1924 which hauled the ultimate Belle in July 1967 ? It was renumbered under the TOPS scheme to 47247 then to 47655 and finally to 47810 and today, January 2013, after 50 years of mainline service, remains operational being one of 33 of the class available for operation on the national network being used by DRS (Direct Rail Services) for freight, stock movements, charter trains and spot-hire duties.

Nine Elms Duty No 33 (Summer 1954) Saturdays Excepted. 8P (MN class) Bournemouth Belle		
	Nine Elms	11.35 a.m.
11.53 a.m.	Waterloo	12.30 p.m.
2.52 p.m.	Bournemouth West	
	Branksome	
	Bournemouth West	4.34 p.m.
6.50 p.m.	Waterloo	7.23 p.m.
7.35 p.m.	Nine Elms	
Saturdays only		
	Nine Elms	12.01. p.m.
12.15 p.m.	Waterloo	12.30 p.m.
2.52 p.m.	Bournemouth West	
	Branksome	
	Bournemouth West	4.34 p.m.
Up to 11 September		
6.50 p.m.	Waterloo	7. 53 p.m.
8. 3 p.m.	Clapham Jn.	
	Nine Elms	-
18 September only		
6.50 p.m.	Waterloo	7.32 p.m.
7.42 p.m.	Clapham Jn.	
	Nine Elms	-

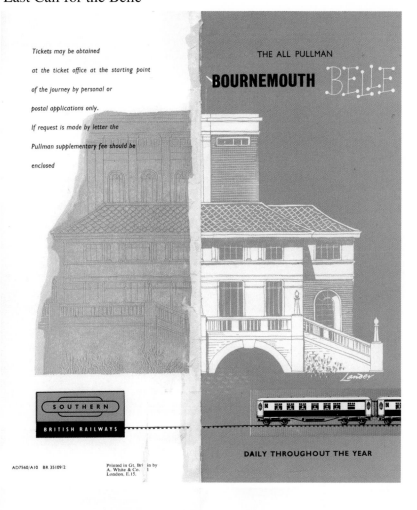

Opposite bottom - A group of railway enthusiasts talk to the driver of Brush Type 4 (later Class "47/0") 2,750hp Co-Co No.D1924 in BR two-tone green livery departing Waterloo with the last "Bournemouth Belle" Pullman to Bournemouth 09/07/67 (Hugh Llewellyn)

Alleviating the post-war gloom of austerity, 21C19 "French Line CGT" passes Vauxhall resplendent with the wooden headboard carried only in 1946/47 consisting of three lines of yellow letters edged in black on a green background. (Rail Photoprints)

Before being ousted from its traditional terminus of Bournemouth West, the Up Belle prepares to depart on a very wet 8th. June 1965 behind No 35030 "Elder Dempster Lines". The train consists of many more vehicles than just the Pullman Brake and Mk1 full brake. The latter were used as replacements after the former Pullman vehicles had been withdrawn. Legend has it that Charles Long, who then worked for Pullman, happened to see a WR full-brake at Clapham Junction one lunchtime around the time replacements were needed. He made arrangements to 'borrow' two such vehicles from the WR, the intention being to retain a similar colour scheme for the whole train. On the whole this was continued through to 1967 although if one of the chocolate and cream vans were not available it was not unknown for a maroon or green variant to be substituted. It was perhaps appropriate that the all-Pullman train should pass into history on the same day as the motive power, for which it was so long associated, Southern steam, for there was no place for the privileged few in the egalitarian world of the new electric dawn.

The Belle leaves Bournemouth Central passing the shed with 35012 "United States Line". During the 1950s, Pullman stock used for the train had gradually evolved from 12-wheel vehicles to more modern 'K' type cars.
Derek Fear

BESIDE THE NORTH DOWNS

A photographic review of the Redhill to Guildford line

Peter Tatlow

(The author trained and worked as a civil engineer on British Railways, Southern Region from 1957 to 1968 and all photographs are by him.)

Having obtained a line-side photographic permit for non-electrified lines from the Public Relations and Publicity Office two floors down from my drawing office in the Waterloo station buildings, the nearest steam-operated line to home in Horsley (Surrey) was the Redhill to Guildford line just the other side of the North Downs and an easy cycle ride on a Saturday morning. Several trips were made in the first half of 1959.

The South Eastern Railway shared the route from London due south through the Coulsdon/ Merstham gap in the Downs as far as Redhill with the Brighton line. Here the SER's original main line turned almost due east to Tonbridge, Ashford, Folkestone and Dover. It also threw out a line due west towards Dorking and through another gap in the North Downs at Guildford, from where it made its way north-west to Reading, there making connection with the Great Western Railway and its lines for the west and north. Although it meant a reversal at Redhill, this line was an incredibly useful way of circumnavigating London,

which was so clearly demonstrated in May/June 1940 when urgently clearing Allied troops landed on the south-east coast following their evacuation from Dunkirk.

Running along the southern flank of the North Downs between Redhill and Guildford, the foothills made for some significant gradients, up which heavy trains struggled to climb to the summit a mile and a half east of Gomshall. This was particularly severe heading west with the four miles at 1 in 100/96 from Deepdene in the Mole Valley with a brief respite through Dorking Town. In the other direction there was a short downhill stretch running into Gomshall in otherwise a steady 1 in 100/96 from a mile east of Shalford, culminating in a final 1 in 96 to the summit.

By the late `fifties, there was still a regular passenger service and substantial goods traffic, all steam-hauled. The ex-SECR 4-4-0s I had seen in the early `fifties, when each Monday afternoon during the summer term the school rifle club visited the Westcott rifle range between the

Left - On a bright frosty morning on 3 January 1959, No. 31628, one of the larger-wheeled Maunsell class 'U' 2-6-0s, with a heavy west-bound goods train is still blowing off when within sight of the summit of the line between Dorking Town and Gomshall.

Right - The local passenger service between Redhill and Reading, via Guildford at approximately the same location with the ridge of the North Down in the left background on 28 March 1959 behind sister 'U' class No. 31622 and a four-coach train

line and the escarpment to fire 0.303 rifles from the 200 and 500 yard firing points, were no longer usual on the line, although one was seen at Tonbridge. Maunsell's 'N' and 'U' class 2-6-0s, on the other hand, were common fare by 1958, particularly on the passenger turns, together with the occasional ex-GW 43xx class and BR Standard class 4 moguls. 4-6-0 S15 class were to be found on heavy freight, with 0-6-0 Maunsell Qs and Bulleid Q1s adding a helping hand with lighter trains. By mid-July 1959 the first phase of the Kent electrification was soon releasing displaced larger locomotives, such as 4-6-0 'King Arthurs' and later 4-4-0 'Schools' class to work out their mileages before all steam was withdrawn from the Region as a whole by July 1967.

Most goods traffic was working right through from Redhill and beyond to Guildford, from where the trains either continued to Reading, or took the Pompey line up to the West of England main-line at Woking. Every week there were at least two heavy trains of ballast hoppers from Meldon Quarry, near Okehampton in Devon, with stone for Brighton and Ashford district engineers' track renewal programmes. The only notable intermediate traffic will have been lime products from the Dorking Greystone Limeworks Co, which was at the end of a long siding up from Betchworth station. From the early sixties freight traffic had begun to fall off, or was routed elsewhere and with the decline of steam on the Southern Region, diesel locomotives, often hydraulic Type 3s, began to take over the passenger turns. In 1965 a number of 3-car diesel-electric multiple units were created when a few spare sets of the flat-sided Hastings were split up and the first two coaches married up to the slightly wider driver/trailer of an electric multiple-unit to create the 'Tadpoles'.

Above - Having nearly completed walking his length one Saturday morning, the permanent way ganger stands back at Dorking Town station, as the smaller-wheeled Maunsell N class Mogul No. 31825 continues its climb past the starting signal on the 1 in 100 gradient, soon to steepen to 1 in 96 with a train of empty ballast wagons on the same day.

Opposite top - Soon afterwards Maunsell's version of a Urie 4-6-0 S15 class No. 30837 drifts down the hill with an east-bound freight, including a number of containers, for Redhill and beyond on 28 March 1959. Note the home signal already restored to danger.

Bottom - Returning back up the hill in the sunlight the same morning, 'King Arthur' class No. 30795 Sir Dinadan struggles as it crawls up the gradient near the village of Westcott with a long west-bound freight train somewhere near the rifle range.

Opposite top - U class No. 31630 has surmounted the summit and coasts down past an intermediate block signal towards Dorking with a goods train for Redhill etc.

Opposite bottom - Approaching the climax the now preserved Maunsell 'N' class No. 31874 has another heavy freight train firmly in its grip as it approaches the summit - known to some loco-men as 'Rest and be thankful'.

This page - Spanning the cutting at the actual summit is the unique, now replaced, Deerleap road bridge with a timber deck supported on three girders each consisting of a series of inverted cast-iron triangular frames tied together at the bottom apex by wrought iron ties.

Above - Over on the other side of the summit No. 31837 with steam to spare gently lets its long train, including four 20-ton Presflos, down the 1 in 100 gradient as it approaches Chilworth station on 2 May 1959. The driver will be hoping the level crossing gates at the station and Tangley Crossing are opened in time for the signal to be pulled off and permit a clear run through to Shalford Junction.

Opposite top - 10 The same day No. 31799, with another of the regular ballast train return workings to the Southern's stone quarry at Meldon, has just surmounted a mini-summit at Shere Heath between Gomshall and Chilworth. The quarry, near Okehampton in Devon, supplied the Engineer's relaying gangs across the Region

Opposite bottom - The Great Western's incursion into Southern territory with Mogul 43xx class heading the north-bound 'Continental'. This was the daily inter-regional through train to and from Margate and Ramsgate on the Kent coast, Hastings and Brighton, via Redhill where it reversed, before going on to Guildford, Reading, Oxford, Birmingham Snow Hill, Shrewsbury to Chester and Birkenhead. Here No. 6324 hauls a train headed by three BR Mark 1 coaches as they pass under the Shere to Peaslake/Cranleigh road over-bridge on 2 May 1959.

Memories of journeys from Guildford to Reading
(known as 'The Rattler')

Viv Orchard

In October 1952 I joined British Railways as a Signal & Telegraph Apprentice at Reading. I lived with my mother at Guildford so this entailed travelling most days on 'The Rattler'. I never found out why the trains between Guildford and Reading were so called. In my view the trains had no more rattle than any others but there was plenty of variety as my diaries reveal and these go back to 1951.

19.2.51. Journeying to Reading found N15 class No. 30455 *Sir Lancelot* shunting at Ash at 6.48am and it was there every morning that week.

At Reading South No. 34104 *Bere Alston* was shunting at 7.33am.

.8.51 Amazingly N15X class No. 32328 *Hackworth* was on the 6.30am dep. Guildford to Reading South. I thought this class was banned from this line!

6.11.52 Colour came back to Reading South as M7 class No. 30241 was seen at 4.15pm still in malachite green livery.

29.4.53 A stranger was in the camp at Guildford in the form of LMS design No. 42074 of 74A depot.

4.5.53 The Godalming goods was seen at 6.06am with E4 class No. 32487.

12.5.53 At Reading South found an un-identified 'Britannia' class probably en route to Nine Elms as the 'Merchant Navy' class had been withdrawn following a crank pin failure.

13.5.53 N15 class No. 30455 *Sir Lancelot* appeared again at Guildford.

25.5.53 No. 34104 *Bere Alston* appeared again at Reading South on the 5.34pm passenger train to Redhill.

27.5.53 N15 class No. 30752 *Linette* was on the 6.0 am Redhill to Reading South passenger train known affectionately as 'The Parly'.

On the same day D class No. 31075 was observed at Reading South decorated in connection with Queen Elizabeth II Coronation.

At Guildford LMS No. 42078 & No. 34089 *602 Squadron* were resting.

29.5.53 Once again No. 30752 *Linette* appeared again on the 6.0am Redhill to Reading South passenger train.

3.6.53 An odd move was observed, albeit not steam, when at 10.20am an EMU Race Special arrived from Aldershot into Platform 4. The Driver changed ends and backed into the Chalk tunnel then ran via Platform 3 to Epsom.

9.6.53 A change of 'Arthur' as No. 30781 *Sir Aglovale* appeared on the 6.0am Redhill to Reading South passenger train.

15.6.53 Royal standby engine U class No. 31800 was immaculate at Guildford.

19.6.53 Another change in 'Arthur' for the 6.0am Redhill to Reading South passenger train: this time No. 30456 *Sir Galahad*.

10.7.53 A rare carriage sighting was the Invalid saloon S7919 an ex-Royal train saloon on the front of the Margate to Birkenhead (Woodside) at Reading General at 1.05pm. This train was known as 'The Conti'.

12.10.53 D class No. 31075 worked the 5.05pm Reading South to Guildford passenger After standing by at Guildford this then worked forward to Cranleigh and back.

Another D class worked the 5.39pm Reading South to Redhill passenger.

At Guildford was C2X class No. 32449 still with Southern style number on back of tender.

15.10.53 Found E3 class No. 32456 hauling a push-pull train from Guildford to Horsham at 8.45am.

20.10.53 A rare sight was E2 class No. 32100 at Guildford at 6.30am.

21.10.53 L12 class No. 30434 on the 4.20pm Reading South to Redhill passenger.

23.10.53 L12 No. 30434 was on the 5.15pm Guildford to

No 31618 at Dorking Town on the 9.45 am Reading to Redhill, 15 December 1962.

Leslie Sandler

Reading South.

9.11.53 N15 class No. 30751 *Etarre* was shunting at Ash also on 10th & 11th.

11.11.53 Unusually M7 class No. 30246 was on the 5.15pm Guildford to Reading South passenger.

12.11.53 An H class No. 31310 was on a Guildford to Horsham passenger.

N15 class 30751 *Etarre* was shunting at North Camp.

13.11.53 N15 class No. 30751 *Etarre* was shunting at Ash.

23.11.53 M7 class No. 30324 was working bunker first on the 6.30am Guildford to Reading South passenger.

27.11.53 M7 class No.30675 on the 6.30am Guildford to

Reading South passenger.

M7 class No. 30026 on the 8.10am Guildford to Reading South all week.

3.12.53 Interesting coaching stock. Matchboarded 'birdcage' brake 3581S ex-Set 901 in bad condition at Guildford.

7.12.53 M7 class No.30675 on 6.30am Guildford to Reading South passenger.

E6X class No. 32411 on the Norwood Goods at Guildford in afternoon.

8.12.53 M7 class No. 30675 on 6.30am Guildford to Reading South passenger.

D class No. 31488 + S15 class No, 30503 + D1 class No.

'U' No 31616 arriving at Shalford on Sunday 11 June 1962 with the 3.35 pm Redhill to Reading.

R S Greenwood

31721 + N class No. 31823 all coupled together passing through Reading General having turned around the triangle due to Reading South turntable out of action. Hence M7 engines working on line.

9.12.53 M7 class No. 30246 on 6.30 Guildford to Reading South passenger.

10.12.53 LMS tank No. 42068 at Reading South with 1.31pm Redhill to Reading South passenger. The stock was worked out by M7 class No. 30374 (72A) as the 3.35pm Reading South to Guildford passenger.

12.12.53 M7 class No. 30027 working Reading South/ Redhill passenger trains.

Once again C2X No. 32449 at Guildford with Southern style number on tender back,

17.12.53 H class No. 31311 (75B) on passenger from Redhill at Reading South (1.33pm dep?). Stock formed 3.25pm to Redhill.

18.12.53 E5 class No. 32591 (70D) was station pilot at Guildford.

4.5.54 BR No. 73035 at Reading South.

7.5.54 BR No. 76054 on 3.50pm Reading South to Redhill passenger.

27.6.55 E2 class No. 32102 at Guildford.

30.7.55 BR No. 76060 on Reading General to Margate relief.

28.2.57 Engine: U class No. 31798. Load: 3 x 31 = 93 tons tare.

Guildford:	7.08am
Wanborough:	7.17pass
Ash:	7.21/7.21 ½
North Camp:	7.25/7.26 ½
Farnborough Nth:	7.30/7.30 ½
Blackwater:	7.35/7.35 ½
Sandhurst Halt:	7.39/7.39 ½
Crowthorne:	7.43 ½/7.44
Wokingham:	7.49/7.50
Earley:	7.56 pass
Reading South:	8.00am.

13.2.57 Engine: M7 class No. 30246 Load: 4 x 31 = 124 tons tare.

Guildford:

Wanborough:
Ash:
North Camp:
Farnborough Nth:

Blackwater:	9.22 ½ pm.
Sandhurst Halt:	9.26/9.26 ½
Crowthorne:	9.30 ½/9.31
Wokingham:	9.36/9.36 ½
Winnersh Halt:	9.40 pass
Earley:	9.42 pass
Reading Spur:	9.44 ½
Reading South:	9.47pm.

1.3.57   Engine: C class No. 31723 Load: 3 x 31= 93 tons tare.

Guildford:	7.50am .
Wanborough:	8.2/8.2 ½.
Ash:	8.9/8.14 ½ *
North Camp:	8.19/8.19 ½
Farnborough Nth:	8.24/8.24 ½
Blackwater:	8.30/8.30 ¼
Sandhurst Halt:	8.34 ½/8.35
Crowthorne:	8.40/8.40 ¼
Wokingham:	8.48/8.49**
Winnersh Halt:	8.53 ½/8.54
Earley:	8.58 ½/8.59 ½
Reading South:	9.08am .

*Stopped for 'Blow up': unable to keep brakes off.

** Contemplated exchanging engines with No. 31621 shunting but decided to go on.

11.2.57 Engine: D1 class No. 31246 Load: 3 x 31 = 93 tons tare

Guildford:	7.05am.
Pinks Hill	7.12
Wanborough:	7.14 pass
Ash Junction	7.16 ½
Ash:	7.18/7.19 ½
Aldershot Junc N	7.21 ½
North Camp:	7.23/7.24
North Camp Sdgs	7.26
Farnborough Nth:	7.27 ½/7.28
Blackwater:	7.32 ½/7.33
Sandhurst Halt:	7.36 ½/7.37
Crowthorne:	7.41/7.41 ½
Wokingham:	7.47/7.48 checked by home signal.
Earley:	7.53 pass
Reading Spur	7.56
Reading Junc	7.57 checked by signal.
Reading South:	7.58 ½

4.3.57   Engine: BR4 No. 80146 Load: 3 x 31 = 93 tons tare

Guildford:	7.16am.*
Wanborough:	7.19 pass**

BR Class 4 No 76058 on a Guildford to Redhill service passing Betchworth, 18 June 1956.

Martin Galley

U class No 31790 leaving Betchworth: no doubt the permanent way gang are relieved to be able to take a few moments break. The BR Mk1 coaches are formed into set No 533.

Ash:	7.28/7.28 ½.
North Camp:	7.32/7.34
Farnborough Nth:	7.37/7.38
Blackwater:	7.42 ½/7.43 ½
Sandhurst Halt:	7.47/7.47 ½
Crowthorne:	7.50 ½/7.51
Wokingham:	7.56 ½/7.57 ½
Winnersh Halt:	8.0/8.0 ½.
Earley:	8.03 pass
Reading South:	8.11am.

*6.0am ex Redhill arrived late and took water. ** checked signals

5.3.57 Engine: BR4 No. 80146 Load: 3 x 31 = 93 tons tare

Guildford:	7.09am .
Wanborough:	7.16 pass
.Ash:	7.19/7.19 ½
North Camp:	7.23/7.24
Farnborough Nth:	7.27 ½/7.28
Blackwater:	7.32/7.32 ½
Sandhurst Halt:	7.35 ½/7.36
Crowthorne:	7.39/7.40 ½
Wokingham:	7.45/7.46 ½
Winnersh Halt:	7.49 pass
Earley:	7.51 pass

Reading Spur	checked signals: 2mins early.
Reading South:	7.59am.

6.3.57 Engine: BR4 No. 80146 Load: 3 x 31 = 93 tons tare

Guildford:	7.06am .
Wanborough:	7.12 ½ pass
Ash:	7.16 ½/7.17 ½
North Camp:	7.21 ½/7.22 ½
Farnborough Nth:	7.26/7.27
Blackwater:	7.31 ½/7.32
Sandhurst Halt:	7.35/7.35 ½
Crowthorne:	7.40/7.40 ½
Wokingham:	7.45/7.46 ½
Winnersh Halt:	7.50 pass
Earley:	7.51 ½ pass
Reading South:	7.58 am.

7.3.57 Engine: BR4No. 80146 Load: 3 x 31 = 93 tons tare

Guildford:	7.05am.
Wanborough:	pass
Ash:	7.15 ½/7.17 ½
North Camp:	7.22/7.23*
Farnborough Nth:	7.26 ½/7.27
Blackwater:	7.31/7.31 ½
Sandhurst Halt:	7.34/7.35

Crowthorne: 7.38 ½/7.39
Wokingham: 7.44 ½/7.45 ½
Winnersh Halt: 7.48 pass
Winnersh Halt: 7.48 pass
Earley: 7.50 pass
Reading South: 7.54am: (2mins early).
* checked at home signal.

9.3.57 Engine: C class No. 31723 Load: 3 x31 = 93 tons tare
Guildford: 7.50am .
Wanborough: 7.59/7.59 ¼
Ash: 8.05/8.05 ½
North Camp: 8.09 ½/8.10
Farnborough Nth: 8.14/8.16*   .
Blackwater: 8.20 ½/8.21
Sandhurst Halt: 8.24/8.24 ½
Crowthorne: 8.28/8.29
Wokingham: 8.34/8.34 ½
Winnersh Halt: 8.39 ¼ pass
Earley: 8.43/8.43 ½
Reading South: 8.49am.
*Driver & Guard talking.

12.3.57 Engine: BR4 No. 76062 Load: 3 x 31 = 93 tons tare?
Guildford: 7.07am .
Wanborough: 7.14 pass
Ash: 7.18 ½/7.10
North Camp: 7.23/7.24
Farnborough Nth: 7.27 ½/7.29
Blackwater: 7.32/7.33
Sandhurst Halt: 7.36/7.37
Crowthorne: 7.41/7.41 ½
Wokingham: 7.47/7.48
Winnersh Halt: 7.51 pass
Earley: 7.53 pass
Reading South: 7.58 ½

13.3.57 Engine: BR4 No. 80146 Load: 4 x 31 + 10(van = 134tons tare
Guildford: 7.07am
Wanborough: 7.14 pass
Ash: 7.18/7.19 ½*
North Camp: 7.23 ½/7.24 ½
Farnborough Nth: 7.28/7.28 ½
Blackwater: 7.32 ½/7.33
Sandhurst Halt: 7.36/7.37
Crowthorne: 7.40 ½/7.41
Wokingham: 7.47/7.48
Winnersh Halt: 7.51 pass
Earley: 7.53 pass
Reading South: 7.58am
* Waiting connection from Aldershot.

14.3.57 Engine: BR4 No. 80146 Load: 4 x 31 + 10(van) = 134tons tare
Guildford: 7.07am
Wanborough: 7.14 pass

Ash: 7.17 ½/7.18
North Camp: 7.21 ½/7.23
Farnborough Nth: 7.26 ½/7.27
Blackwater: 7.31 ½/7.32   .
Sandhurst Halt: 7.35/7.36 ½.
Crowthorne: 7.40/7.41
Wokingham: 7.46/7.47
Winnersh Halt: 7.50 pass
Earley: 7.52 pass
Reading South: 7.57 am.

23.4.57 Engine: T9 class No. 30705 Load: 3 x31= 93tons tare
Guildford: 7.50am
Wanborough: 7.59 ½/8.00
Ash: 8.05/8.05 ½
North Camp: 8.09/8.09 ½
Farnborough Nth: 8.13 ½/8.14
Blackwater: 8.19/8.20
Sandhurst Halt: 8.23/8.23 ½.
Crowthorne: 8.27/8.28
Wokingham: 8.33/8.35
Winnersh Halt: 8.39/8.39 ½.
Earley: 8.43/8.43 ½.
Reading South: 8.49 am.

27.5.57 Engine: GWR 73XX No. 7317   Load: 10 x 31= 310tons tare
Reading General: 1.38pm.
Reading Junction: 1.40 pass.*
Reading Spur: 1.41 pass
Earley: 1.44 ½ pass
Winnersh Halt: 1.47 pass
Wokingham: 1.49 ½ pass**
Crowthorne: 1.53 ½ pass
Sandhurst Halt: 1.55 ¼ pass
Blackwater: 1.57 pass
Farnborough Nth: 1.59 ½ pass
North Camp: 2.2 ¼/2.4
Ash: 2.08 pass
Wanborough 2.11 ¼.pass
Guildford 2.17pm.
*via Old Bank.
** PSR 30mph

29.5.57 Engine: LMS class 4   No. 42088   Load: 108tons tare
Guildford: 7.04am .
Wanborough: 7.10 pass
Ash: 7.13/7.14 ½
North Camp: 7.17 ½/7.19 ½
Farnborough Nth: 7.22/7.23
Blackwater: 7.27/7.28
Sandhurst Halt: 7.30 ½/7.33 ½
Crowthorne: 7.35 ½/7.37 ½
Wokingham: 7.42/7.43 ½
Winnersh Halt 7.46 pass.
Earley 7.47 ½

'S15' No 30836 coasts into Betchworth with the 6.3 pm Redhill to Reading service on 19 April 1963.

G D King

Reading South:	7.51 ½am.	Sandhurst Halt:	7.35 ½/7.36 ½
		Crowthorne:	7.39 ½/7.40
2.4.57 Engine: Q class No. 30533 Load: 113 tons tare		Wokingham:	7.45/7.47
Guildford:	7.07am .	Winnersh Halt:	7.50 pass
Wanborough:	7.15 pass	Earley:	7.52 ½ pass
Ash:	7.19/7.20 ½	Reading South:	7.57am.
North Camp:	7.24 ½/7.26		
Farnborough Nth:	7.24 ½/7.30	12.4.57 Engine: BR4 No. 76058. Load: 130 tons tare	
Blackwater:	7.34 ½/7.35 .	Guildford:	7.04am.
Sandhurst Halt:	7.38/7.38 ½	Wanborough:	7.11pass
Crowthorne:	7.42/7.42 ½	Ash:	7.14/7.14 ½
Wokingham:	7.47 ½/7.48	North Camp:	7.18/7.20 ½
Winnersh Halt	7.51 ½ pass	Farnborough Nth:	7.24/7.24 ½
Earley	7.54 pass	Blackwater:	7.28 ½/7.29
Reading South:	7.59 am.	Sandhurst Halt:	7.32/7.33
		Crowthorne:	7.37/7.38
8.4.57 Engine: N class No. 31862 (pilot) + Q class No.		Wokingham:	7.43/7.44
30533. Load: 100 tons tare		Winnersh Halt:	7.47 ½ pass
Guildford:	7.07am.	Earley:	7.49 ½ pass
Wanborough:	7.15pass	Reading South:	7.54am.
Ash:	7.18/7.19		
North Camp:	7.23/7.24	18.4.57 Engine: BR4 No. 76057 Load: 10 bogies. 400	
Farnborough Nth:	7.27 ½/7.27 ¾	tons gross.	
Blackwater:	7.32/7.32 ½	Reading New Jn:	1.18 ½.pm.

Earley:	1.25 pass	Wokingham:	7.46/7.46 ½
Winnersh Halt:	1.27 pass	Wokingham:	7.46/7.46 ½
Wokingham:	1.30 pass*	Earley:	7.51 ½.pass
Crowthorne:	1.34 pass	Reading South:	7.57 ½.am.
Sandhurst Halt:	1.36 pass		
.Blackwater:	1.37 ½ pass		
Farnborough Nth :	1.40 pass		
North Camp:	1.43/1.44 ½.		
Ash:	1.50 pass		
Wanborough:	1.52 ½ pass		
Pinks Hill:	1.54 ½ pass		
Guildford:	2.00 ½ pm.		

29.7.57 – 2.8.57 LMS 4 2-6-4T No. 42067 working 6.0am Redhill to Reading South.

26.8.57 An EMU oddity. 4-LAV 2947 on 7.01am Guildford to Portsmouth.

10.7.57	Engine: BR4 76056	Load: 148 tons gross
	Guildford:	7.08am .
	Wanborough:	7.15 pass
	Ash:	7.18 ½/7.19
	North Camp:	7.22/7.24
	Farnborough Nth:	7.27 ½/7.28
	Blackwater:	7.32/7.32 ½
	Sandhurst Halt:	7.36/7.36 ½
	Crowthorne:	7.40/7.40 ½

4.9.57	Engine: WC class No. 34047 *Callington*	Load:
	155 tons gross	
	Guildford:	7.05am
	Wanborough:	7.13 pass
	Ash:	7.16 ½/7.17
	North Camp:	7.21/7.22
	Farnborough Nth:	7.26/7.27
	Blackwater:	7.31 ½/7.32
	Sandhurst Halt:	7.35/7.36
	Crowthorne:	7.39/7.39
	Wokingham:	7.46/7.47

Through working. The Margate to Birkenhead service with No 31798 on GW stock at Shalford East Lane crossing, 1 May 1950.
E C Griffiths

Eastbound cattle special at Gomshall Lane Level Crossing behind No, 76060, 4 August 1956. J Spencer-Gilks

Winnersh Halt:	7.50 pass
Earley:	7.52 pass
Reading Spur:	7.54 pass (checked
signals)	
Reading Junc:	7.56 pass (checked
signals)	
Reading South:	7.58 ½.am.

5.9.57   Engine: WC class No. 34047 *Callington*   Load: 155 tons gross

Guildford:	7.06am.
Wanborough:	7.13 pass
Ash:	7.16 ½/7.18
North Camp:	7.22/7.23
Farnborough Nth:	7.27/7.27 ½
Blackwater:	7.32/7.32 ½
Sandhurst Halt:	7.36/7.36 ½
Crowthorne:	7.40/7.41 ½
Wokingham:	7.46 ½/7.48 (checked
signals)	
Winnersh Halt:	7.51 pass
Earley:	7.52 ¾ pass
Reading South:	7.57 ½.am.

2.1.58   Engine: BR class No. 73083 (73A) Load: 148 tons gross

Guildford:	7.08am.
Wanborough:	7.16 pass
Ash:	7.19 ½/7.21
North Camp:	?
Farnborough Nth:	7.30/7.30 ½
Blackwater:	7.35½/7.36
Sandhurst Halt:	7.39/7.39 ½

Crowthorne:	7.43 ½/7.44
Wokingham:	7.49/7.50
Winnersh Halt:	7.53 pass
Earley:	7.55 pass
Reading South:	7.58.am.

14.4.58   Engine: Q class   No. 30533 Load: 100 tons tare

Reading South:	6.52pm
Earley:	6.57 pass
Winnersh Halt:	6.59 pass
Wokingham:	7.02 ½/7.03 ½
Crowthorne:	7.08 ½/7.09 ½
Sandhurst Halt:	7.13/7.14
Blackwater:	7.17/7.18
Farnborough Nth:	7.23/7.24
North Camp:	7.27 ½/7.28 ½
Ash:	7.34 ½/7.35
Wanborough:	7.40/7.40 ½
Guildford:	7.48pm.

8.5.58   Engine: M7 class No,30321 Load: 150 tons gross

Guildford:	7.05am .	
Wanborough:	7.16 pass
Ash:	7.20/20 ½
North Camp:	7.24 ½/7.25
Farnborough Nth:	7.29½/7.29 ¾
Blackwater:	7.34½/7.35
Sandhurst Halt:	7.38½/7.39
Crowthorne:	7.43 ½/7.44
Wokingham:	7.49 ½/7.50
Winnersh Halt:	7.53 ½. pass
Earley:	7.56 pass
Reading South:	8.02.am. (checked

signals)

9.5.58 M7 class No. 30321 on 6.0am Redhill to Reading South.
V class No. 30909 *St Pauls* on 6.0am Redhill to Reading South.

20.11.58 Engine: V class No. 30909 *St Pauls*   Load: 100 tons gross

Guildford:	7.08am
Wanborough:	pass ?
Ash:	7.19 /7.20
North Camp:	7.23 ½/7.25
Farnborough Nth:	7.28/7.28 ½.
Blackwater:	7.32/7.35
Sandhurst Halt:	7.38/7.38 ½
Crowthorne:	7.42/7.43 ½
Wokingham:	7.48/7.48 ½
Winnersh Halt:	7.52 pass
Earley:	7.54 pass
Reading Junction:	7.59/8.0 ½ (signals)
Reading South:	8.03am. (signals)

24.11.58-27.11.58   V class No. 30909 *St Pauls* on 6.0am Redhill to Reading South.

28.11.58 Engine: V class No. 30909 *St Pauls* Load: 120 tons gross

Guildford:	7.06am
Pinks Hill	7.11 ½.pass
Wanborough:	7.13pass
Ash Junction:	7.15 pass
Ash:	7.16 ½ /7.17
Aldershot Jn Nth:	7.19 pass
North Camp:	7.20 ½/7.21 ½
North Camp Sdgs:	7.24 pass
Farnborough Nth:	7.25 ½/7.25 ¾
Blackwater:	7.30/7.30 ¾
Sandhurst Halt:	7.33 ½/7.34 ½
Crowthorne:	7.38/7.39
Wokingham:	7.44 ½/7.45 ¼
Winnersh Halt:	7.48 ½. pass
Earley:	7.50 ¼ pass
Reading Spur	7.52 ½ pass
Reading South:	7.55am.

Peasmarsh Junction (south of Guildford). 'D' class 4-4-0 No 31744 in what was then being described as 'LNWR livery' - actually BR Black, with the 6.34 pm Guildford to Cranleigh. 21 July 1950. (This service had commenced as the 5.05 pm Reading to Guildford and was booked for a 30 minute wait upon arrival at Guildford.)
P M Alexander

The 1.58 pm Reading to Redhill approaching Shalford a5 3.0 pm on 1 May 1950, behind E class No 31516.

E C Griffiths

12.12.58 , 13.12.58, 15.12.58.   V class No. 30909 *St Pauls* on 6.0am Redhill to Reading South.

V class No. 30902 *Wellington* on 5.5pm Reading South to Guildford.

N15 class No. 30795 *Sir Dinadan* at Reading South.

2.1.59 – 17.1.59 V class No. 30902 *Wellington* on 6.0am Redhill to Reading South.

6.0am Redhill – Reading South delayed 60mins due to point failure at Gomshall.

N15 class No. 30795 *Sir Dinadan* on 6.0am Redhill – Reading South.

7.4.59   Engine: T9 class No. 30732 Load: 97 tons tare
Reading South: 8.50pm.
Earley: 8.55 pass

Winnersh Halt:	8.57 pass
Wokingham:	8.59½/9.01 ½.
Crowthorne:	9.07/9.08 ¾.
Sandhurst Halt:	9.12/9.14 ½.
Blackwater:	9.17 ½/9.18
Farnborough Nth:	9.22 ½/9.23 ½
North Camp:	7.28/7.29 ½.
Ash:	7.33 ½/7.34
Wanborough:	7.38/7.38 ¼
Guildford:	7.46pm (checked
signals).	

8.4.59   Engine: T9 class No. 30732 Load: 97 tons tare

Reading South:	8.50pm.
Earley:	8.54 ½ pass
Winnersh Halt:	8.56 ½ pass
Wokingham:	8.59½/9.02
Crowthorne:	9.07 ½/9.09 ½
Sandhurst Halt:	9.13 ½/9.14
Blackwater:	9.17/9.17 ¾

Farnborough Nth:	9.22 ½/9.24
North Camp:	9.28 ½/9.30 (stopped by
home signal)	
Ash:	9.34 ½/9.35
Wanborough:	9.38¾/9.39
Pinks Hill	9.41 ¾ pass
Guildford:	9.45 ½ pm.

3.6.59 N15 class No. 30796 Sir *Dodinas le Savage* on 5.55pm Guildford to Reading South.
N15 class No. 30795 *Sir Dinadan* on goods train at North Camp at 6.25pm.

6.6.59 Engine: N15 class No. 30796 *Sir Dodinas le Savage* Load: 93 tons tare

Guildford:	7.06am
Pinks Hill	7.12 pass
Wanborough:	7.14 pass
Ash:	7.17/7.18
North Camp:	7.21 ½/7.22
Farnborough Nth:	7.26/7.26 ½
Blackwater:	7.31/7.31 ½
Sandhurst Halt:	7.35/7.35 ½
Crowthorne:	7.39/7.40
Wokingham:	7.45 ½/7.47
Winnersh Halt:	7.51. pass
Earley:	7.53. pass
Reading South:	7.55am.

8 & 9.6.59 LMS 2-6-4T on Birkenhead – Margate at Reading General.

10 & 12.6.59 N15 class No. 30795 *Sir Dinadan* on 6.0am Redhill to Reading South.

10.5.60 Engine: 700 class No. 30308 Load: 161 tons gross

Guildford:	7.05am
Pinks Hill	7.10 ½ pass
Wanborough:	7.13/7.13 ¼*
Ash Junction:	7.16 ¼. pass
Ash:	7.17 ¾/7.18 ¼
Aldershot Jn Nth:	7.21 pass
North Camp:	7.23/7.23 ¾
North Camp Sdgs:	7.26 pass
Farnborough Nth:	7.27 ¾/7.28 ¼
Blackwater:	7.33/7.34
Sandhurst Halt:	7.37/7.38
Crowthorne:	7.42/7.42 ¼
Wokingham:	7.48/7.48 ½
Winnersh Halt:	7.52. pass
Earley:	7.54. pass
Reading Spur	7.56 ½ pass
Reading Junction:	7.57 pass
Reading South:	7.58 ½am.

* stop by mistake. (pre-empting new timetable?)

29.7.60 Engine: V classs No. 30914 *Eastbourne*. Load: 11 x 31= 341 tons tare Driver: D. Curd (Redhill)

Reading General:	1.29pm
Reading Spur:	1.32 pass
Earley:	- pass
Winnersh Halt:	1.38 ¼ pass*
Earley Up IBS:	1.40 ½ pass*
Wokingham:	1.43 ½.pass**
Crowthorne:	1.48 pass
Sandhurst Halt:	1.51 Pass
Blackwater:	1.52 pass
Farnborough Nth:	1.55 pass ***
North Camp:	2.00/2.01 ½
Aldershot Nth Jn:	2.04 ¾ pass
Ash:	2.06 pass
Ash Junction:	2.08****
Wanborough	2.10 pass
Pinks Hill:	2.12 ½. Pass
Guildford	2.17pm

* checked to 5mph.
** 30mph PSR.
*** checked to 15mph.
**** 15mph TSR.

28.3.62 BR No. 73112 on 7.10am Guildford to Redhill also on 5.30pm Reading Southern to Clapham Yard vans.

11.4.62 SR Ferry PMV S2S with raised Guards lookout at Reading Southern.

SR Ferry PMV S3S with raised Guards lookout at Reading Southern.

*K class No. 32343 beautifully turned out in lined black at Guildford at 7.0am.

17.9.62 *K class No. 32345 very clean at Reading Southern. * same engines?

(No-one under the age of 55 will really remember just how plain bl**dy cold the winter of '62/'63 was! ED.)

The following extracts all record events during the long, bitterly cold winter of '62/'63.

6.0am Redhill to Reading Southern ran via Down Goods Loop at Wokingham due to points failure at junction.

14.1.63 WC class on 2am Dover to Reading Goods from Redhill: also 9.27pm Reading South to Redhill and 5.27pm London Bridge to Reading Southern. 7.24am Reading Southern to London Bridge but taken off at Redhill as out of coal!

As per 14.1.63 but taken off at Guildford.

As per 14.1.63 but taken off at London Bridge as so much escaping steam driver could not see shunter!

Mogul back on Reading Southern to London Bridge. Unrebuilt WC at Reading Southern awaiting coaling. Advised 6.0am Redhill to Reading Southern is now an S15 turn although one has not yet appeared!

18.1.63 Engine: U class No. 31633 Load: 128 tons tare

Guildford:	7.15am*
Wanborough:	7.22/7.23
Ash:	7.28/7.29
North Camp:	7.32/7.32 ½.
Farnborough Nth:	7.36/7.36 ½.
Hawley Down IBS:	7.40/7.41 ½.
Blackwater:	7.44 ½/7.45
Sandhurst Halt:	7.48 ½/7.49
Crowthorne:	7.53/7.53 ½
Wokingham:	7.59/7.59 ½**
Winnersh Halt:	8.03 ½ pass
Earley:	8.06 pass
Reading Spur	8.09 ½ pass
Reading Junction:	8.10 pass
Reading Southern:	8.11am.

*Late departure due to 6.35am left at 7.00am & 6.50am at 7.10am!
**Checked at Home signal.

23.1.63 6.00am Redhill to Reading Southern arrived 16 mins. late at Guildford and taken off train due to bad steaming of U class engine No. 31638. Replacement engine Q1 class No. 33025 left MPD for Yard SB at 7.30am behind the engine for the 7.50am Guildford to Reading Southern! Was thus trapped on Engine line. No. 33025 arrived on train at 7.55am. The 7.50 Guildford to Reading Southern was still in sidings with its engine. No. 33025 had steam heat pipes frozen and hence no steam heat on train. Weather very cold with thick fog.

Up Portsmouth EMUs were being diverted to Platforms 3 and 8 and many passengers missed trains as there was no station announcer! Guard of delayed 6.00am Redhill to Reading Southern, now with engine No. 33025, was reluctant to leave Guildford without steam heating but Station Inspector insisted as too much time already lost!! Train left without any heating and ice on inside of windows. Why did not MPD check that heating pipes were working?

Engine: Q1 class No. 33025 Load: 128 tons tare

Guildford:	7.57am .	
Wanborough:	8.05/8.05 ½	
Ash:	8.10/8.11	
North Camp:	8.16/8.16 ½*	
Farnborough Nth:	8.20/8.21	
Blackwater:	8.25 1/8.26	
Sandhurst Halt :	8.29 ½/8.30 ½	
Crowthorne:	8.33 ½/8.35**	
Wokingham:	8.39 ½/8.41	
Winnersh Halt:	8.44. pass	***
Earley:	8.46 ½ pass***	
Reading Spur	8.49 ½ pass****	
Reading Junction:	8.50 pass	
Reading Southern:	8.52am	

*Checked at Home signal.
**Train packed solid with 6 people standing in 1st. class compartment. Very cold,
no heating and ice on windows and mirrors.
***This train was running in the path of the 7.50am from Guildford which stops at
Winnersh Halt for school children and at Earley for business people at Whiteknights Park.
They were all carried on to Reading Southern!!!
****Checked at Home signal.

PS. It transpires that the 7.50am Guildford to Reading Southern was eventually cancelled. So why wasn't the engine on that train used in place of No. 33025 at Guildford? 9.25am Reading Southern to Redhill cancelled as no stock!

5.05pm Reading South to Guildford consisted of one Maunsell side corridor coach plus one BR open corridor coach plus one LMS bogie luggage van. There was no 1st. class, no heating (very cold) and one corridor door window completely missing! There was a FOR REPAIRS card dated 22.1.63 issued at Tonbridge on the running board concerning the window.

24.1.63 5.05pm Reading Southern to Guildford has same stock as 23/1/63.
6.35am Guildford to Reading Southern departed 7.00am.
6.50am Guildford to Ascot EMU departed from Platform 5 instead of 8 at 7.10am.
7.05am Guildford to Reading Southern held until 7.18am waiting for Ascot EMU to clear. Why?
7.05am could have left on time and stopped at Wanborough thus allowing Ascot EMU to run non-stop to Ash and gain a few minutes. Wanborough passengers could change at Ash. During this very bad weather the working of this line would be better if Blackwater signal box was open and thus reduce the long Block sections. This would be better that having Farnborough North open.

7.05am Guilford to Reading Southern departed at 7.18am due to no platform staff to unload mails and give right away.

30.1.63 Engine: N class No. 31866 (bearings & journals badly worn) Load: 100 tons tare

Guildford:	7.05am
Wanborough:	7.12/7.12 ½
Ash:	7.17/7.17 ½
North Camp:	7.23/7.23 ½
Farnborough Nth:	7.28 ½/7.42 ½*
Blackwater:	7.46 ½/7.47
Sandhurst Halt:	7.50/7.50 ½
Crowthorne:	7.53 ¾/7.54
Wokingham:	7.59/7.59 ½**
Winnersh Halt:	8.02 ½ pass
Earley:	8.04 ½ pass
Reading Spur	8.07 pass **
Reading Junction:	8.07 ½ pass

No 31798 leans to the curve at Ash Junction with another Birkenhead to Margate working, this time with a GWR Hawksworth coach as the lead vehicle. The line to Tongham and Farnham diverges to the left. 1.50pm, 7 September 1949.

Reading Southern: 8.08 ½am.
*Held by signals. 6.35am Guildford to Reading Southern had stopped at North Camp with
No. 31627 for a blow up. Waiting for long Block section from Farnborough North to Wokingham to clear. Driver recovered 2 mins. on run to Reading Southern
**Checked by signals.

6.2.63   Weather good. 7.03am Guildford to Reading Southern left at 7.07am from Platforms 6&7 late due to Ascot EMU late from sidings which also had to depart from Platform 5 due to van being left in Platform 8.
7.05am arrived at Ash at 7.21 ½ and left at 7.25 waiting connection from Ascot EMU.
Arrived at North Camp at 7.29 Guard talking to station staff. Apparently changing trains at
Crowthorne and concerned about late running. Farnborough North arrived at 7.34 and
departed 7.35 once again Guard talking to station staff.
Arrived Crowthorne at 7.47 ½ and
Guard changed trains to 7.27am Reading Southern to London Bridge. Departed at 7.51 and
arrived at Reading Southern at 8.08am.

7.03am Guildford to Reading Southern stopped at North Camp Home signal at 7.22 departed at 7.23 ½ being flagged into platform. Unable to lock level crossing and thus release Home signal due to road grit put down on ice on road getting into level crossing gate bolt. Departed station at 7.25 ½. No time made up to Reading Southern.

13.2.63 Engine: S15 class No. 30847 Load:2+van= 72tons tare

Guildford:	7.05am
Pinks Hill	7.11 ½ pass
Wanborough:	7.14/7.14 ½
Ash Junction:	7.17 pass
Ash:	7.19/7.19 ½
Aldershot Jn Nth:	7.21 ½
North Camp:	7.23 ½/7.24
North Camp Sdgs:	7.26 pass
Farnborough Nth:	7.28/7.28 ½
Blackwater:	7.33/7.33 ½
Sandhurst Halt:	7.36 ½/7.37
Crowthorne:	7.41/7.41 ½
Wokingham:	7.47/7.47 ½
Winnersh Halt:	7.51pass
Earley:	7.33 pass

Tender first passenger working. No 31862 pulling out of Betchworth with what is probably a Redhill to Dorking 'short working', 25 July 1956. *Martin Galley*

Reading Spur	7.55 ½ pass
Reading Junction:	7.56 ½ pass
Reading Southern:	7.57 ½am.

According to Driver this S15 was the only serviceable loco left at Redhill. 15 stopped for repairs! Also advised that the Bulleid pacifics diagrammed for the Reading Southern to London Bridge service and return had been shelved. This S15 was not due to the note of 17.1.63.

7.03am Guildford to Reading Southern departed at 7.0am (early!) Emergency stop as right-away given with van doors open! (Platforms both sides) New right-away given with 2 passengers on platform with one trying to get on. 2 minutes early! Passed Pinks Hill distant 'On' at 7.06am . Checked Pinks Hill home signal running close to 6.50am EMU to Ascot. My time was right to clock on Guildford Platform 8 and also at Wanborough. Departed Wanborough at 7.10am. Train lights turned off at 7.50am (not light enough to read).

Heat turned off at Wokingham arrived at Reading Southern 7.56am. Apparently a replacement Guard had taken over at Guildford. Still dark and cold in train.

20.2.63 7.03am departed Guildford at 7.04am. Once again steam heat turned off at Wokingham! Checked at Winnersh Halt and Earley arrived Reading Southern at 8.01am very cold.

Success too late!

Q1 No. 33019 in Up Sidings behind Guildford Yard signal box coupled to all stock for pre-heating. This is the first time pre-heating has taken place. Pity as although a heavy frost during night the morning was one of the mildest for months. If only this had happened during the bad weather there would have been warmer trains, fewer damaged water tanks and frozen fittings. There would have been less FOR REPAIRS or NOT TO GO labels and even unmoveable

The 2.31 pm Redhill to Reading between Dorking and Gomshall on 26 June 1956. No 33022 is piloting 'U' No 31800.
J Head

stock. Due to stock shortage many 4-car Maunsell corridor sets have been split to provide 2 x 2-car sets. This means that either the train is a composite + 2nd. brake or a 2nd. only + 2nd. brake. Which can mean no 1st. class. In some cases the train has been just a 2nd. corridor + a guard's luggage van and in some cases a fitted goods brake van. Only one train is consistently good and this is the 6.0am Redhill to Reading South which is nearly always warm and clean and often has more modern Bulleid or BR Standard corridor stock. The 7.48am Guildford to Reading Southern and the following train from Dorking Town; also the 5.05pm Reading Southern to Dorking Town are very poor for stock. Always very dirty and badly maintained. Probably due to lack of cleaning facilities in its roster. Little done at Reading Southern, only EMU done at Guildford and nothing at Dorking Town. Very few Maunsell Sets have antimacassars in the 1st. class. The seats are solid with dirt. Woodwork is dirty and smoke engrained. Windows are rust covered from brake blocks. Drop lights are often without handles causing delay in exit and longer station times. Light bulbs are often missing. Only about a quarter work. Compartments should have one ceiling light and four reading lights. Reading lights seldom work. Lamp shades are often missing or on the luggage racks or are swinging precariously on their fittings. The old SECR lamps usually had water slopping around in them! Washing facilities seldom exist. During cold weather water tanks are emptied to stop freezing. There are no towels or soap. Wash basins are filthy and often contain a collection of loco ash via the ventilators. The WC basin has a large gaping hole through which one can see the track and

a howling draught comes up it! Seldom any water in this department. There appears to have been a reduction in obscene writing on the walls. These observations concern the 1st. class. It is assumed the 2nd. class is the same. With the split Maunsell sets there can often be too great a proportion of 1st. class. As a result many 2nd. Class ticket holders travel in 1st. class even though there is room in the 2nd. People prefer to travel in their own compartment rather that with others. Perhaps they have to behave then! There is only need for one smoker 1st. class and one non-smoker 1st. class. Downgrade the rest to 2nd. There are seldom ticket collectors and when they do appear they are so obvious no one gets caught. What is needed is clean, well-maintained stock. No need for more modern types. Today the 6.0am Redhill to Reading Southern was withdrawn at Reading Southern because the Guard complained of lack of heat in his van despite the passenger accommodation heating being fine. There was an argument between the C&W examiner and the Station Inspector about putting a green FOR REPAIRS label on the stock. Surely if something needs repair then a FOR REPAIRS label should be attached. There was no need to take the stock out of service.

27.2.63 No pre-heating of stock at Guildford this morning. That idea didn't last long!

Engine: S15 class 30847 Load: 5 x 31 = 155 tons tare.
(Maunsell 2nd. brake+composite+2nd.brake+composite+2nd.)
    Guildford: 7.03am .
    Pinks Hill   7.09 ½ pass

'V' No 30925 'Cheltenham' approaching North Camp with the 3.35 pm Reading to Redhill, 30 June 1962.

D B Clark

Wanborough:	7.11 ½./7.12
Ash Junction:	7.15 pass
Ash:	7.17/7.17 ½
Aldershot Jn Nth:	7.19 ½
North Camp:	7.21 ½/7.22
Farnborough Nth:	7.25 ½/7.26 ½
Blackwater:	7.30 ½/7.31 ½
Sandhurst Halt:	7.35 ½/7.36
Crowthorne:	7.39 ½/7.40 ½*
Wokingham:	7.45 ½/7.46
Winnersh Halt:	7.49pass
Earley:	7.51 ½ pass
Reading Spur	7.54 ½ pass**
Reading Junction:	7.56 pass **
Reading Southern:	7.57 ½am.

*Waiting passengers running to station.
**Checked by signals. Stock ex 6.35am Guildford being cleared from platform.
Heating 50lbs/sq " from engine but so many leaks second coach was only luke-warm.

No.31813 ex-works on 6.0am Redhill to Reading Southern. No modified front end but fitted AWS.

BR No. 82015 on Redhill to Reading Southern at Wokingham at 5.15pm.
Nos.31613, 31800, 30836 & 82017 all ex-works on Redhill – Reading Southern line.
No. 82017 at North Camp at 5.45pm.

No. 30835 on 6.0am Redhill to Reading Southern.

6.08am Reading Southern to Redhill with steam & diesel (pilot) locos. Steam for heating only!

Q class No. 30543 on Redhill to Reading Southern passenger at Farnborough North at 6.20pm.

No. 45346 (16B)* on 6.0am Redhill to Reading Southern passenger.

Q class No. 30542 on Reading Southern to Feltham goods at Wokingham.

18.9.64 No. 45299* on Redhill to Reading Southern passenger at Farnborough North at 6.25pm.
Q class No. 30542 on previous passenger.

*Engines have had top lamp iron moved to side of smokebox therefore carry old head code of disc at either end of buffer beam rather than one disc at chimney which is the current head code for this route. (Margate to Reading)

Ex-LNER B1 class No. 61313 on 12.05pm Reading Southern to Redhill passenger. Was at Redhill following failure on a troop train. Repaired and running in or pinched.

Driver ?.Olive (Redhill). Engine U class No. 31873.

6.00am Redhill to Reading Southern passenger.
Arr. Guildford 7.05am. Right time to Wokingham home signal where near stand. Checked to Winnersh Halt where stopped by signal for 1 min. Slow run to Earley home signal where checked also at starter and advanced starter signals. Slow run to Reading Southern checked at all signals. Signal failure at Wokingham advanced starter and down IBS.

Stock: Set 466. 2nd. brake S4441S (ex boat train stock) + composite S5631S* + 2nd. brake S4063S*+ composite S5133S*.
*Maunsell stock.

17.11.64 Loco: BR No. 73113 *Lyonesse.*   Stock: Set 771 (SBK+compo+SBK)

6.00am Redhill to Reading Southern. Left Guildford on time. Checked by signals at North Camp. Waiting passengers at Crowthorne. Checked by signals at Wokingham. Dead stand at Winnersh Halt by signal. Checked by signals at Earley.
Reading Southern arr. 4 mins. late. Good spirited run with loco worked out. Loco leaking steam badly from injector pipe by cab window. Stock very good condition and clean. Learned today that 5.5pm and 5.47pm from Reading Southern to be cut out in January. Ridiculous! New service is basically 24mins past each hour from Reading. How many people leave work at 5pm compared with 5.30pm? Look at mad rush for 5.47pm now! Also why precede the electrics at 28mins past each hour? Assume Guildford services will be all stations. Might as well close line down! New stock will be maintained at St. Leonards!

18.11.64 Loco: N class No. 31403. Driver: Gabriel (Redhill) Stock: 3 coach Set 55.
6.00am Redhill to Reading Southern.
Guildford depart 7.03am and right time to Wokingham Home signal where dead stand for 3 mins. Passed Starter 'On' as Track Circuit failure. Checked at Winnersh Halt by signals. 8 mins. late at Reading Southern. Down preceding EMU late every morning this week and always given preference at Wokingham Junction. Hard work by Guildford line loco crews wasted. Engine worked well. Stock good and clean.

19.11.64 Engine: U class No. 31804. Driver: Rambler? (Redhill) Train: 100 tons tare.
7.50pm Reading Southern to Redhill. Departed at 8.25pm. The 8.50pm left at 9.15pm.
Engine for 8.50pm brought stock in for the 7.50pm. Hence was not released until 8.25. Then to shed for turning, water, etc.
Wokingham dep 9.25pm. Good engine working. Driver trying to make up time. Checked at Ash to near stand at Home signal due to level crossing. Wanborough dep 9.53pm. Guildford arr 9.59pm.

'The Bug' - Mr Drummond's Private Saloon

W Eaton

(Reproduced from 'Trains Illustrated Annual' with grateful thanks to Ian Allan)

In my younger days on the then London & South Western Railway, I had the interesting experience of being the regular fireman on Mr. Dugald Drummond's famous saloon, which was stabled at Nine Elms and known to all and sundry as "The Bug." The late Chief Inspector James was the driver. He was quite fearless, and he needed to be, for his Chief had a pronounced taste for speed.

For the benefit of readers who know nothing of the subject of this article, let me say that it was no locomotive antique which had had some superannuated coach tacked on to it for inspection purposes. This unique combined engine and coach, specially designed by Drummond, appeared brand new from Nine Elms Works in 1898. The locomotive itself was a single-driver with driving wheels 5 ft. 7 in. in diameter; it had a leading bogie with 2 ft 6 in. wheels, and a trailing bogie of longer wheelbase which supported the cab and the short saloon adjoining it. The whole thus made a 4-2-4 wheel arrangement; it measured 35 ft. 7 in. over buffers and weighed 37 tons in running trim.

Chimney and dome, the latter with safety-valves above, were typically Drummond; the boiler had a heating surface of 550 sq. ft, and the little firebox a grate area of 11.3 sq. ft; working pressure was 175 Ib. per sq. in. This boiler was nicely proportioned to supply two outside cylinders 11 in. diameter by 18 in. stroke. About 1,000 gallons of water could be stored in the side-tanks, and the coal bunker, inside the cab, held a ton. "The Bug " was built for speed, and could certainly show its paces on the slightest provocation.

Mr. Drummond, in his capacity as Locomotive, Carriage and Wagon Superintendent (as the Chief Mechanical Engineer was then known), used his saloon for visiting all the out-station locomotive depots, and in his journeys he covered every stretch of line on the old South Western system. It enabled him, for instance, to travel from London to Eastleigh Works and back within a few hours, or to visit Exeter in a day with a comfortable margin of time to do business at that end of the line.

The saloon was cleaned daily at Nine Elms, and an experienced cleaner was allocated to this work. Our usual orders were to arrive at Surbiton station at 9.0 a.m. sharp. Mr. Drummond would come from his residence nearby, settle down in the saloon, and off we would go, sometimes for a short trip to Portsmouth and sometimes to the far West. We were always well prepared with food, in case we should have to "lodge " for a night.

I remember one occasion when we had been down the North Cornwall line. We were on our way back to London and were held up by a goods train at Ashbury, near Okehampton. It was seven o'clock in the evening, and as it was so late Mr. Drummond decided that he would stay the night at Exeter. A message was to be sent forward to book him a room at an hotel. This was before the days of telephones, and Ashbury Station had a single-needle telegraph instrument, which the only porter on duty was quite incapable of manipulating. Enquiries for the stationmaster or the booking clerk revealed that they had gone that evening to a Farmer's Hunt Supper.

The "Old Man" started to read the Riot Act, whereupon I suggested that, having had experience of telegraph instruments when a lad in the Traffic Department, I might be able to save the situation. His comment to me was, "You're not such a fool as you look!" Anyway, he got his room at the hotel that night, and James and I lodged in the enginemen's dormitory.

Talking of goods trains, there was a hatchway between the saloon and the engine footplate through which orders were transmitted to the driver. If our pace was too leisurely - that was below 60 m.p.h., Drummond would shout out, "What's the matter, James. D'ye think this is a goods train? "

One day, an official of the old Highland Railway was staying with him. We took them both to Eastleigh Works and afterwards to the South Western Hotel at Southampton for lunch To give us a clear run back, it was arranged that our return journey should be made ahead of a Bournemouth express, which was due away from Southampton Central Station (then called Southampton West) about 2.40 p.m. We therefore left at 2.30 p.m. Before starting, Drummond came on the footplate, looked at my fire with the remark, " That's verra good," and told James darkly that the Highland gentleman was to be given the run of his life !

We went like a whirlwind. After racing up to Basingstoke, we ran the 23 miles from Basingstoke to Woking in 16 minutes by stop-watch, an average of 85 m.p.h! As both engine and saloon together had but five axles on a short wheelbase, the saloon seemed to skip across the points and crossings like a horse jumping a gate! Anyway, the sensation of passing over the junction at the west end of Weybridge Station was the last straw for the Highland man. Coming to the hatchway, he implored James to moderate the speed. As we were then approaching Surbiton, his wish was gratified, but Mr. Drummond enjoyed the joke hugely.

In my time the saloon was fitted with two brake blocks only, on the driving wheels. This meant that the brake power was none too good, and in a tight corner it was necessary to put the engine into reverse. Once when running down into Ilfracombe we nearly came to grief. James had stopped at Mortehoe to examine his sand gear, to make sure we should be able to keep the saloon safely under control down the 1 in 36 gradient into Ilfracombe ; but after we started away a shower came on, and we just could not avoid hitting the buffer-stops a hearty smack. "Drum," who had risen from his seat to alight, was bumped down again by the impact, and we expected a storm. However, when he saw that no damage had been done, and remembered that James had stopped as a precaution at Mortehoe, he said little. But on the next trip to Ilfracombe he ordered a vacuum-braked coach to be attached in rear on the journey, for additional brake-power, although on the climb to Mortehoe this nearly stalled the little single-wheeler, which was not used to being harnessed to other vehicles !

Drummond had the reputation of being something of a tyrant and slackness he could not stand. However, he was always very kind to me, possibly because I was "the boy," and when he observed my overalls in a filthy state - from raking out the ashpan, I told him - he gave me a golden sovereign with instructions to buy two new pairs at once. A similar sum came my way when he heard that I had become the father of twins, with instructions to "put it in the bank."

The fireman's duties on "The Bug " were very exacting. Everything had to be just right. No coal dust was tolerated, and every piece of coal was hand-picked, broken into convenient lumps and carefully stacked in the rather inadequate bunker space. This part of the preparation work would often take me two hours, and I used to be on duty early for the purpose. On the road I also acted as "steward." Those were the days of luncheon baskets, which one could

order in advance, to be available at certain principal stations. "Drum " always had two baskets: one had to contain a bottle of lemonade and the other a bottle of "Bass."

There was also a carafe of water in the saloon and in the Exeter area this had to be filled from a particular tap which supplied spring water. One day he saw me returning from the tap, and as I held up the glass to the light - the water was pure and clear - I ventured to remark that it would be "nice with a drop of something in it, knowing his liking for "Scotch." He said, "You don't want any of that, do ye? " To which I replied, "No, I'm teetotal, Sir." He could be affable with those he knew would not disrespect his position, but woe betide any man who tried to argue with him!

Occasionally, "The Bug " was used by various traffic officers. I remember we were taking a few of them to Salisbury when two springs broke with a loud report underneath the saloon while we were approaching Andover at high speed. These springs had broken before, so we carried on, knowing that we should come to no harm. What the occupants thought we never discovered; probably it was put down to loose ballast or something similar. But I think they preferred to travel by ordinary train after that!

Mr. Drummond died in 1912, and that was the end of the saloon's meteoric career, although it survived to become a Docks Inspection Car at Southampton, and only recently has been broken up at Eastleigh Works..

'The Bug'. According to Bradley, the vehicle ran some 171,304 miles between January 1900 and December 1912, equivalent to almost 1,100 per month. The thought of travelling at an average of 85 mph over the 16 miles from Basingstoke to Woking hardly bears considering, especially as the only brakes were on the driving wheels. The porthole for communication between the saloon and cab may be seen.

The EPB Story Part 3: The Double-Decker

David Monk-Steel

(Part 1 appeared in SW20 and Part 2 in SW24)

The Concept

The double-decker was a brave, but unsuccessful, experiment in the search by the Southern Railway for increased capacity to handle the business traffic into London without incurring huge capital costs.

By the late 1930s capacity had become a problem again. Plans were developed for new 'six-a-side' stock, using welded all-steel bodies, the option to extend trains to ten cars was also considered, and if World War Two had not intervened, would have been well in hand in the mid - 1940s. The new pre-war 4-SUBS squeezed people into compartments only 5' 6" between walls, and although 938 persons could sit in a full train, the standing passengers, who were a significant feature of the business trains, found it very uncomfortable. Wartime conditions tended to stifle

Opposite and above - Full size mock up of a section of a DD coach on display and used for publicity purposes. Might the views have been taken on different occasions - witness the lighter interior colour scheme? It was usual for staff from the various offices to be drafted in and used as 'passengers' on such occasions. Marylebone, February 1949.

The Italian 'Double-deck motor 'bus.

Motorbuses in Rome. [*Photos. by H. A. Venton, Paris.*]

An Italian Method of Packing Passengers.

SPACE ECONOMY ON 'BUSES IN ROME.

The photographs above show two of the omnibuses operated by the City of Rome Transport Department.

The picture on the left is that of an electric bus used for local town traffic. As will be seen, its general appearance bears a very strong resemblance to that of a tramway car.

The vehicle in the right-hand photograph is of particular interest, both as to its unusual length and ingenious interior arrangements.

The orthodox omnibus stairway is dispensed with, the top deck being reached in an unusual manner.

The upper and lower saloons consist of a series of compartments with seats face to face divided by a centre gangway raised about nine inches above the floor of the lower saloon

A diagram of the seating arrangement of the 'bus illustrated on right.

compartments. The ceilings of the latter form the seat portions of the upper deck compartments, the upper deck floors falling between the seat backs of the lower deck to give leg space.

On entering the vehicle the passenger finds himself on the raised centre gangway, and merely steps down when he wishes to travel in the lower saloon.

Should he wish to make use of the top deck he steps up to it by means of a couple of notches or rungs inset in the bodywork immediately below the floors of the upper deck compartments.

It will readily be seen that owing to the fact that the passenger is already raised nine inches above the floor level and that the top deck compartments are fairly low, it is not at all a difficult matter to negotiate the upper deck.

Nevertheless, a vehicle of this description would not be very suitable for town work, and

the omnibus in question, which was only built last April and is, therefore, still in the experimental stage, is used for town sightseeing and journeys into the suburbs involving few stops. The seating capacity is about 100.

overt criticism; usually these were met with the riposte, "Don't you know there's a War on!" This new train appeared in 1941 and marked the end of new construction until the cessation of hostilities.

World War Two held up the process of expansion, and apart from the reformation of the old wooden sets to standardise on four-car set formations, no more new sets appeared until 1946. The new post war '4-SUBS' had more room for standing, with compartments 6' 1" between walls, and eventually standard sets appeared with centre gangways that allowed circulation within the coach, and thus even more room for standees.

Eight-car, six-a-side stock did not solve the problem, so the Southern Railway started to evaluate the other options. One option requiring expensive capital investment in both trains and the infrastructure was to adopt ten-car train working. A further 66 new two-car sets would be required, but worse still virtually every platform would need to be lengthened from 515' to 675', with associated alterations to track, signalling and some bridges. To compound this, the power supply system would not be able to cope with the extra load, and would require considerable replacement and strengthening. Faced with this problem the Southern Railway's CME Mr. O V S Bulleid came up with one of his revolutionary ideas, the double-decker! He made reference to this in a paper read to the British Association in the summer of 1948 and there was speculation in the railway pPress, but formal announcement did not come until early in 1949.

Construction

Anyone with knowledge of the Southern Railway's Eastern Section will be familiar with its tight loading gauge. The saga of the Hastings line is well known, and the North Kent route was also riddled with loading gauge restrictions. The idea of a double-decked train on this route would therefore seem preposterous. Bulleid was not a man to let such trifles stop him. His ideas

were ingenious. It is most likely that he got the idea of an interlocking upper and lower deck from Italy, and an article showing a sightseeing motor 'bus operated by the City of Rome Transport department using a very similar arrangement of seats appeared in the Southern Railway Magazine as early as September 1931 (p 317), prophetically, however, the article states " a vehicle of this description would not be very suitable for town work ...is used for town sightseeing and journeys into the suburbs involving few stops!".

In Bulleid's design maximum use was made of the loading gauge by using small wheels, lowering the floor and taking the roof to the limit, by eliminating as best possible those things that required space outside the body shell. Ventilators were made long and thin. The upper deck

windows were sealed shut. Commode handles were dispensed with. Foot boards were omitted, except under the driver's and guard's van door.

These innovations did not come without cost, and to try to compensate for the reduced natural ventilation, (and the increased demand for it too!) pressure ventilation was installed. The powered ventilator units were located in cupboards underneath the floor of the top deck, with external, top hung doors to enable access from the outside. These drew air up from beneath the carriage and out under the feet of passengers on the top deck. In theory this increased the air flow to the passengers, but former occupiers of the upper deck will testify that this was not always a resounding success.

Despite the inclusion of a step plate at the threshold

Trail run for the first set, No 4001.

with the helpful words "Mind the Gap" cast in to it, the absence of foot boards contributed to the increase in the number of persons falling between train and platform, and in service between 18th November 1949 and 23rd November and again between 6th January 1950 and 20th June 1950 a total of 19 reported cases of persons falling between train and platform, and a further two cases of persons falling on to the platform from the train, were recorded against these prototype sets.

The absence of commode handles exacerbated the boarding and alighting hazards and also caused problems with doors flying open in the carriage washing machines. Before the prototype train was washed all the doors that opened facing the direction of travel had to be locked by depot staff.

The special small wheels caused problems too, and cracks in the wheel caused the set to be temporarily withdrawn for modification soon after introduction.

A wooden mock-up of the prototype was made to test public reaction, and was displayed at Marylebone in February 1949. Much was made of it in the contemporary press, and even Roland Emmett celebrated it in one of his delightful cartoons.

Lancing built the train during the summer of 1949. It consisted of two four-car units each 257' 4½" over buffers. The welded steel underframes were of standard length (62') and centre buffer/coupled in standard Southern style. The intermediate buffing gear was at a lower level than normal to match the reduced floor height, but the buffers at the outer ends were standard heavy-duty SR pattern. The solebars of the motor coaches were fabricated from two different height sections (10" & 15") to enable conventional height buffing at the outer end. The 15" solebars occurred beneath the guard's and driving compartments where normal height accommodation was required. The height from rail to roof was 12' 9" (4½" greater than contemporary 'normal' stock), The body was 9' 0" wide at the waist but was slightly wider at the bottom and tapered slightly inwards from bottom to top. The tare weight was given as 39 tons for a motor coach, and 28 tons for a trailer. This tonnage was the same as the latest 4-SUB unit, but whereas the 4-SUB seated 386 persons, a four-car double-decker seated 508, with a further 44 on tip up seats under the top deck windows, if they desired. Passengers

4-DD Set 4001 ex-works when brand new, probably at Brighton. This BR official picture is posed with four officials (can anyone identify who is who?) but there are no other details accompanying the print. Note too that the control jumper is situated centrally, but following some mistakes when coupling, this was repositioned to the 'secondman's' side, the original holes being plated over.

BR Official / D. Monk-Steel collection

could also stand upstairs or down and frequently did.

The trailers' bogies as originally fitted were much modified from the normal electric type. Each had 8' 0" wheelbase, and the wheels were 3' 0" diameter. The side frames were depressed and there was no swing plank bolster. Side bearers were provided transferring the weight directly on to the bogie framing. The wheels were originally welded BFB type, but these developed faults and were eventually replaced with a more conventional type. Early in use these bogies also seem to have been replaced with a more conventional arrangement of secondary suspension, and this probably happened during the second period of withdrawal in 1949. Photographs in March 1950 show swing plank bolsters in situ under the trailer bogies.

Motor bogies were a modified version of the standard SR motor bogie with 8' 9" wheelbase and 3' 2" diameter wheels. Each carried two 250hp English Electric lightweight type 507 traction motors.

The two sets were fitted with Westinghouse Brake of a novel type to the Southern because it was electro-pneumatically operated. Experiments had been conducted in 1947 with electro-pneumatic brakes on two sets of Brighton / Hastings Express stock, which appears to have

been successful, but was not perpetuated and was removed. A set of the equipment therefore became available at just the right time to be incorporated into the new train. Train wires in the control circuits operated air valves that controlled the air in the brake cylinders very precisely. These sets were the fore-runner of the next generation of Southern Electric sets, and almost all the electric multiple-units which derived from them on all regions of BR (except the Western). This self-lapping electro-pneumatic brake was, however, unique to the double deck stock, and thus these eight cars could never run in multiple with any other than their own kind.

The body shell was formed conventionally from light steel sections welded on a jig to thin steel sheet, to form standard panels, all then being assembled and welded on a jig to create an integral unit. These techniques were being used to construct the new all-steel

4-SUBs that were contemporaries to the double-decker. Door details were similar to contemporary stock, although the doors were flat and not curved as on the standard electric suburban stock (4-SUB), and the ventilators, top light, droplight and door catches were similar.

The inner ends were similar to the familiar standard

8-DD departing from Cannon Street on 12 June 1959. Despite there being seats upstairs people can still be seen standing in the downstairs compartment.

The late R.C.Riley

ribbed ends of the 4-SUB units, but to the 4-DD straight-sided profile. Large junction boxes were fitted to the outside of the inner ends, with doors to them located within the adjacent passenger compartment. These were locked with a special key. Jumpers between coaches were coupled into prominent boxes at roof level. Access to the roof was to be had by a series of steps welded to the inner end of the motor coaches with an adjacent tubular handrail.

The driving ends also followed 4-SUB styling, with large fixed windows on driver's, and secondman's side, and a roller blind two-character route indicator between. The driver entered the cab through separate bodyside doors. The controls were similar to the 4-SUB stock: the more modern driving desk to be found in the 4EPBs proper was still two years away. The jumper cabling was slightly different from earlier suburban stock, in that the lighting, brake and traction control was incorporated into the 27-way jumper, and a power jumper separately provided. This former stock had power, lighting and control cables arranged separately. The brake and reservoir hoses were still kept at buffer-beam level, and screw couplings provided between sets. A standard air whistle was provided.

Despite the extra body-height a guard's periscope was fitted, as were some roof mounted conduits. The guard's double doors were inset and a foot-board extended from under the driver's door to the guard's doors.

The passenger seats were narrower (16½" against 18") and the cushions were thinner than those in

contemporary electric stock (3" against 7"). Back rests were thin upholstered squabs screwed to the compartment walls. Much use was made of varnished or painted shaped plywood in the interior. Upholstery covering was similar to the colour and style being used in the 4-SUB series, with a red/brown uncut moquette decorated with outline floral shapes in a lighter colour. During heavy overhaul in February 1958 this was replaced by 'Trojan' dark grey uncut moquette decorated with linear mosaic pattern of coloured squares that was being provided new to the Kent Coast electric stock (4CEP/BEP) at that time. It carried this upholstery up to final withdrawal.

Luggage space was available under the lower deck seats, or above the upper deck seats, and handrails were liberally provided for standees. The stairs were supported on cast alloy units. Aluminium plate was also incorporated into the structure of the interior.

The passenger communication chain was provided above each door, but was absent on the upper deck.

Motor coaches had five lower and five upper compartments, and trailers had seven lower and six upper compartments. Each compartment group had 22 seats, 11 up and 11 down with two tip-up seats on the upper deck underneath the windows. The middle compartment of each trailer did not have stairs, and thus seated 12 persons. Otherwise each upper compartment was reached from one of the adjacent lower ones by a short flight of stairs. When introduced, the compartment adjacent to each guard's van

Set 4002 leads 8-DD on the 4:23 pm Gravesend Central to Charing Cross into platform 4 at London Bridge on 29th April 1954. The wider spacing of the track between platforms 4 and 6 originally accommodated No. 5 through line. Until the station was rebuilt in 1976 express trains to and from Hastings, Ramsgate, Margate or Dover ran fast through London Bridge, and the through line and this line assisted the passage of non-stop trains including the many freight services to the North via the Metropolitan Widened lines. 5 road was lifted to allow platform 6 to be extended to accommodate 10 car trains.

The late R C Riley

Set	Coach	Type	Built		Diagram
4001	S13001S	Motor Brake Third	5 Sept. 1949,	Lancing	2128
	S13501S	Trailer Third	5 Sept. 1949,	Lancing	2021
	S13502S	Trailer Third	5 Sept. 1949,	Lancing	2020
	S13002S	Motor Brake Third	5 Sept. 1949,	Lancing	2128
4002	S13003S	Motor Brake Third	10 October 1949,	Lancing	2128
	S13503S	Trailer Third	10 October 1949	Lancing	2020
	S13504S	Trailer Third	10 October 1949	Lancing	2021
	S13004S	Motor Brake Third	10 October 1949	Lancing	2128

Diagrams 2020 and 2021 were virtually identical, the main difference would appear to be the arrangement of intermediate buffers, and roof conduits and jumper boxes.

was labelled "Ladies Only", and the compartment next to that as "No Smoking". The stair-less compartment in one of the trailers was also "No Smoking", and the third compartment (upper and lower) in the other trailer likewise. The "No Smoking" content increased over time.

Lighting was by special 70v tubular lamps, 6" long, mounted into the seat partitions above the heads of the passengers. Heating was incorporated into the pressure ventilating units, and was thermostatically controlled by the guard. The set was formed as per the table at the foot of the opposite page.

The diagrams 2020 and 2021 were virtually identical, the main difference would appear to be the arrangement of intermediate buffers, and roof conduits and jumper boxes.

Introduction into Service

4001 left works in September 1949 and 4002 in October. A series of proving runs took place on the southern end of the Brighton line. Official photographs show it so employed; the best known was posed just south of Haywards Heath tunnel. The sets were allocated to Slades Green. The whole train was inspected on 1st November 1949 by the press, official dignitaries from Government and members of the Railway Executive, who rode from Charing Cross to Dartford and back. A fault developed on this first run because it was found possible to cross the nose end jumper cables over inadvertently, because the different plugs and sockets were in close proximity to each other. The outcome of this was that the train tried to go the wrong way. During the VIP run it actually backed towards the buffers at Charing Cross by mistake, with the Minister of Transport at the controls! It subsequently became a total failure at Blackheath, until the fitter riding with the train spotted the error and rectified it. This was eventually prevented in future by moving the jumpers from underneath the route indicator to the secondman's side. The train went into public service on November 2nd, 1949 but developed further faults and was withdrawn the following day. It re-

emerged on November 18th but didn't last long in traffic: because of the failure of the welded wheelsets it was again withdrawn on November 22nd. It did not then return to traffic until January 6th 1950 following considerable modification to wheels and bogies.

Working in Service

The routes from Charing Cross and Cannon Street to Gravesend Central via, Dartford (all routes) was given provisional clearance for the train in service, and the route via the Brighton Line to Lancing or Selhurst was available by special arrangement. No other routes were available, and the train could not work in multiple with any other trains.

The service planned to operate during the early 1950s was as shown. *Note that contrary to popular belief that the train always operated as an eight-car train, the diagrams **did** require the train to operate as a four-car set for a period during the day.

The service changed very little over the years, but was gradually reduced in the 1960s.

The Verdict

The train was not a resounding success. Some members of the public didn't like it and some would boycott it and wait for the next service. The complaints arose from the thinner seats, stuffy and cramped top deck, and more worrying, from passengers who felt trapped and vulnerable in the top deck as the train emptied out. There were a few actual reports of assaults, which fortunately did not result in loss of life (although there are apocryphal stories of murders, it has not been proved).

Passengers also fell out of the train or between the train and the platform with alarming regularity. The absence of footboards would appear to have contributed to this. It was slow when loading and unloading, which was a distinct embarrassment at London Bridge and the termini where platform occupation was at a premium.

There were no recorded staff complaints, but additional precautions were needed when dispatching the

	arr	dept	
Slade Green		6.57 a.m.	empty
Barnehurst	7.3 a.m.	7.5 a.m.	via Bexleyheath
Charing Cross	7.42 a.m.	7.50 a.m.	via Sidcup
Crayford	8.23 a.m.	8.30 a.m.	via Sidcup
Cannon Street	9.3 a.m.	9.16 a.m.	via Blackheath and Woolwich (detach 4 cars at Slade Green)*
Dartford	10.2 a.m.	10.9 a.m.	via Sidcup
Charing Cross	10.50 a.m.	10.58 a.m.	via Greenwich
Dartford	11.45 a.m.	12.2 P.M.	empty
Slade Green	12.7 P.M.	2.15 P.M.	(attach 4 cars) empty*
Crayford	2.21 P.M.	2.27 P.M.	via Sidcup
Cannon Street	3.06 P.M.	3.17 P.M.	via Blackheath and Woolwich
Gravesend	4.17 P.M.	4.23 P.M.	via Bexleyheath
Charing Cross	5.28 P.M.	5.35 P.M.	via Bexleyheath
Barnehurst	6.10 P.M.	6.10 P.M.	empty
Slade Green	6.13 P.M.		

train to ensure both safety and punctuality, especially at busy times, and as the door catches could not be relied upon to keep the 'facing' doors closed in the carriage washer, staff had to carriage-key lock one side of the unit each time it had a daily mechanical clean. The train therefore had 'nuisance' value.

A report by C. P. Hopkins, Chief Regional Officer,

Southern Region dated 12th August 1950 to the Southern Region Board weighed all the evidence from the experience gained, and the comparative costs associated with ten-car trains and double-deckers, and concluded that double-deckers were not the complete answer. The double-decker did seem to have great benefits on cost grounds, as can be seen as follows:-

ROLLING STOCK	DOUBLE DECKER	10 CAR TRAINS
DOUBLE-DECKER - 66 eight-car trains plus 4 additional 4 car single deck units	£4,337,661	
10-CAR TRAINS - 66 new 2 car units plus refurbishment of 132 existing 4 car set (underframes and bogies) with new all steel bodies.		£3,557,197
STATIONS AND TRACK		
DOUBLE-DECKER - Platform clearances	£45,000	
10-CAR TRAINS - Extension of platforms at 72 stations, new berthing sidings and signalling alterations.		£1,396,671
POWER SUPPLIES		
The replacement of power supplies by a new 50 Hz system together with the reconstruction of Deptford Generating Station was stated to be needed for the Ten Car Scheme, but was not costed, so presumably would have to be done anyway.		
EXTRA ANNUAL RUNNING COSTS		
Maintenance.	£38,324	£22,300
Staff – Operating.	£4,300	£2,150
Staff - Electrical	£7,500	£900
Power Consumption.	£11,500	£45,250

THE EPB STORY Part 3: THE DOUBLE-DECKER

Opposite page - Set 4002, Driving Motor Brake Third S13004 nearest (note no ownership badge, left hand number and absence of S suffix), stands in Gravesend Central on 2 December 1950. The roller blind has been changed to '46' signifying Gravesend Central to Charing Cross via Sidcup.
The late Denis Cullum

	DOUBLE DECKER	10 CAR TRAINS
ROLLING STOCK		
DOUBLE DECKER - 66 eight car trains plus 4 additional 4 car single deck units.	£4,337,661	
10 CAR TRAINS - 66 new 2 car units plus refurbishment of 132 existing 4 car set (underframes and bogies) with new all steel bodies.		£3,557,197
STATIONS AND TRACK		
DOUBLE DECKER - Platform clearances	£45,000	
10 CAR TRAINS - Extension of platforms at 72 stations, new berthing sidings and signalling alterations.		£1,396,671
POWER SUPPLIES		
The replacement of power supplies by a new 50 Hz system together with the reconstruction of Deptford Generating Station was stated to be needed for the Ten Car Scheme, but was not costed, so presumable would have to be done anyway.		
EXTRA ANNUAL RUNNING COSTS		
Maintenance.	£38,324	£22,300
Staff – Operating.	£4,300	£2,150
Staff - Electrical.	£7,500	£900
Power Consumption.	£11,500	£45,250

It is also interesting to note that of the 72 stations considered for adjustment for double-deck working, the former London Chatham and Dover Railway routes from Victoria to Sevenoaks, the Crystal Palace High Level and London Bridge to Tattenham Corner routes were included. It was positively decided that the double-decker would be employed on race days to shift the crush of racegoers!

Mr. Hopkins prophetically considered the increase in the number of casualties that might occur in the event of a major collision, no doubt with the Purley Oaks, and Battersea Park collisions fairly fresh in his mind. It is terrifying to consider the additional carnage that might have ensued if on the night of 4th December 1957 the 5.18 p.m. Charing Cross to Hayes standing at Parks Bridge M8 signal had been formed of an eight- coach double decker set instead of 10-EPB.

Despite the obvious cost benefits he identified the operating problems and finally suggested that the double-decker was not the ideal solution, and recommended that the ten- car scheme be adopted. It would appear that the Board endorsed this late in 1950 for in early 1951 they made an announcement that no more double - deckers were to be built, and ten car trains were to be answer to their capacity problems.

Normal Service

Despite the decision not to continue with the double-decker concept the Southern Region retained the two sets in service, on the original routes for another twenty years.

The train underwent few changes in its life. The most obvious was the livery. On introduction the livery of malachite green was applied to sides and outer ends, with the application of left hand coach numbers, and large set numbers over each route indicator. The roof was originally silver-grey but darkened to black/brown with age. The inner ends and underframe were painted black. At first there were no ownership markings, but before long right hand numbers and the cycling lion appeared on the sides of each motor coach. Coach numbers alone appeared on the right-hand ends of trailer coach sides. The set numbers were applied in smaller number transfers at about the same time. I n January 1958 the new darker green was applied at Lancing Works, with the British Railways coach emblem that included the lion, now rampant, holding the wheel (Ferret and Dartboard). In the early 1960s a yellow panel was painted on each nose end, and about 1968 the sets appeared with full yellow ends to make them stand out to trackside workers. The sets were re-numbered 4901 and 4902 on 26th

Set 4002, Driving Motor Brake Third S13004 ready to work as part of the formation of a Gravesend Central to Charing Cross via Sidcup service, 11 March 1950.

The late Denis Cullum

September 1970, to free up their original numbers for the new 4-PEP units, which eventually arrived on the Southern in July 1971. The sets were repainted plain rail blue at about the same time.

Other less obvious changes during the 1960s were : the air whistle was replaced by twin roof-mounted air horns at each end, smaller roller blinds were fitted, incorporating red blanks to supplement, and eventually replace tail lamps, spring loaded ice-scraper shoe-gear replaced the gravity shoes, the shoe beams were altered (inverted) at that time to permit a different method of attaching the shoe-gear, the removal of roof-mounted ventilators for the 70v batteries, which were situated under the floor of the upper deck of the "Ladies Only" compartment and which vented through the guard's van roof.

The non-standard nature of the sets, and their general unpopularity with passengers and officials, resulted in the withdrawal on 1st October 1971, having run 700,000 miles. Its last service was the 18.04hrs Charing Cross to Dartford via Bexleyheath on that day.

The train was not scrapped immediately. The coaches were moved firstly to Plumstead, and then to Hoo Junction. Three coaches of 4902 were purchased privately and hauled to Ashford Steam Centre, the rest were cut up on site by Smeeth Metals in November.

Sadly preservation was not permanent, and when Ashford Steam Centre got into difficulties the three coaches were disposed of: the sole surviving trailer S13503 was cut up at Ashford on 15th August 1984, and the motor cars were dispersed. S13003 stayed in Kent. S13004 went to the Northampton Steam Railway, Pitsford, where attempts were made by its new owner to restore it and to fit normal height buffers at the inner end to enable it to be used as hauled stock. After a long period of storage, during which time it suffered badly from vandalism and weather damage, it has once again moved (1999) to another owner and another site at Ironstone Museum, still in Northamptonshire.

Motor coach S13001 of set No 4001 stands in Gravesend Central on 11 March 1950. The slender ventilators associated with the pressure ventilation system and the exposed lighting and control conduits are well illustrated.

The late Denis Cullum

Above left and right - Interior views showing the lower deck plus access to and actual upper deck seating. Clever design had maximised the space but at the cost of limited walking space for passengers.

One of the two 4-D Double-Deck units now clothed in the drab all-over-blue livery adorned with the 'Arrow of indecision' logo. It was captured at Plumstead on 7 October 1971. The immense size of the sets is emphasised in this view which also clearly shows the lack of commode handles and footboards plus the recessed luggage van/guard's compartment. The staggered compartments will also be noted.

Very probably one of the several 'official' photographs of No 337 taken of course on the Crumbles siding at Eastbourne. The engine is in grey with black and white lining and lettering.

The Brighton 'Moguls'

Jeremy Clarke

When, in October 1911, at the age of only twenty-nine years, Lawson Billinton received his official appointment as Locomotive Superintendent of the London, Brighton & South Coast Railway he had held the position on a temporary basis for the preceding eight months due to the indisposition of Douglas Earle Marsh. However, unlike Marsh and his predecessors, he did not take responsibility for the Carriage & Wagon Department, this being at last ceded to Albert Panter. The latter had been appointed General Foreman of the department in 1888 following service with the LNWR at Wolverton and two spells under his father at Eastleigh. Upgraded to Manager in 1904, Panter had served Stroudley, Robert Billinton and then Marsh - under whom he produced some really excellent passenger rolling stock - before finally taking full charge himself. The change possibly occurred because of the department's move to Lancing but was quite as likely due to the late realisation by the Brighton Board that the ever-increasing demands of the combined duties had got beyond the capabilities of one man to administer satisfactorily.

Lawson Billinton took office at a time when industrial relations at Brighton were still in a state of turmoil. Klaus Marx describes Marsh's arrival in 1905 as being '.... like a new injudicious headmaster, intent on implementing fresh ideas'. The problem was that in his enthusiasm for change he did not appear to see anything of much value in the equipment to hand or, more importantly, the staff who used it. Also during his time he was facing the increasing confidence and influence of the Trade Union movement as well as a conservative workforce which constantly challenged change and modernisation. But besides that, Marsh is recorded as being a difficult and taciturn man, reportedly with a degree of 'arrogance, impatience, obduracy and testiness' (Marx). On the other hand he was faced by a Board of Directors which, while deploring the dreadful state of locomotive availability when he took office, apparently failed to understand this was a problem largely of its own making. The Board had constantly refused to sanction the expenditure which would improve that situation on the grounds there weren't any monies to spare. But it seems it took them some time to realise that the cost of engines lying idle out of traffic and not earning was probably greater than that required to rectify the situation.

Almost from his appointment Marsh and, indeed, Robert Billinton before him, had tried to obtain authority to install additional up-to-date machinery in the works and get permission to extend overtime working as well as requesting particularly that more skilled men be employed. Inevitably the Board's hand was eventually forced by the continuing and growing backlog of repairs the works simply could not accommodate, a position reported to the Locomotive Sub-committee in 1908 by Robert Urie who had been called in over Marsh's head to investigate. Here again the Directors absolved themselves of responsibility, happy to blame Marsh for the problem. But by that time he had belatedly

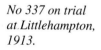

No 337 on trial at Littlehampton, 1913.

No 339 was the third engine of the class, outshopped from Brighton in March 1914. Fitting of the top feed in the second dome occurred in February 1920. The engine is finished in gloss black and lined, probably in red.

been able to begin the reconstruction and reorganisation of the Works at Brighton, in which circumstances the dire repair situation inevitably worsened. Lawson Billinton took a hand here, undertaking some quite heavy repair work at New Cross where he was District Locomotive Superintendent, though that couldn't have made much impression on the overall position.

Apart from his less than agreeable personal traits Marsh's coming from another company, with no previous experience at Brighton, was held against him so far as his workforce was concerned. Lawson Billinton, as will be shown, did not start with this disadvantage. He was the third son and fourth child of Robert and his wife Alice. She was the daughter of Polish immigrants with whom Robert had lodged when he went in 1874 from Brighton to Derby to work for the Midland Railway. Alice's maiden name, Boskovsy or Butzkopfski, was passed on to Lawson as a second given name. Lawson itself came from Robert's interest in motoring, in particular of Harry Lawson, who started out making bicycles but then turned to setting up various companies to do with 'developments' in the infant motor industry. We have to thank him for introducing the annual London to Brighton Veteran car run but in truth he was later found to be a conman of the first order and eventually served a 12-month prison sentence with hard labour for fraud.

Stemming from the time of Lawson's apprenticeship at Brighton under his father and subsequent appointments with the company, many of the men in the Works and on the footplate of Brighton engines already knew him when he took command and, by the same token, he knew them. Mutual trust was therefore established from the beginning of his tenure, the boss having an appreciation of, and regard for, the people who worked for him. Though disagreements continued, there no longer appeared to be such aggressive and debilitating malice between management and men. It is ironic that as an apprentice Billinton's progress reports were written by his father with all the possibilities that brought at least a degree of favouritism and, indeed, of nepotism; though what survives shows no evidence of either. But Lawson already had a good grounding with a theoretical and practical engineering course at Tonbridge School under his belt before entering his apprenticeship in January 1900, together with a mechanical engineering diploma.

Following his apprenticeship, Lawson laboured in various 'shops' in the works before being promoted to draughtsman in 1903. In September that year Robert appointed him Inspector of Materials, sending him to Glasgow to oversee construction of some steel bogie wagons. With that work complete he then found himself superintending oil burning trials on various locomotives

Tender from a 'K' class locomotive recorded at the station end of Brighton Works, circa1921.

The doyen of the class, no 337, again but the picture is a puzzle. Despite the headcode this may well be the four-track section of line between Streatham Common and Selhurst, most probably on the straight stretch from Norbury to Thornton Heath which is largely on embankment. If so the train is on the down main suggesting a Battersea starting point and bound at least for Three Bridges, thereafter maybe Lewes / Newhaven, Chichester or Brighton. The engine is still in LBSCR livery though the wires for the overhead electrification are in place: these were energised on 1st April 1925 but some work had been done before the First World War.

before, in September 1904, becoming Assistant Foreman at New Cross, the Brighton's main London locomotive depot.

Soon after Marsh succeeded the elder Billinton, Lawson was again charged with carrying out experimental work but with a far wider remit that took in almost all aspects of developments on both locomotives and rolling stock. Following a period as Assistant Outdoor Superintendent at Brighton, Billinton returned to New Cross in February 1907, later succeeding the incumbent District Locomotive Superintendent. He was still in charge at New Cross when Marsh's departure on sick leave began.

The year 1911 was a difficult one for industrial relations, particularly in the mines and the docks and on the railways. The national rail strike of that year began in August. But the way Billinton dealt with his people, both

workshop and footplate, may be significant because Brighton men did not join it, though they were encouraged by their Unions to produce a list of grievances for discussion and consideration.

The large number of engines in works or still awaiting repair when Billinton took office – in the region of 30% of the capital stock - and those stored on the scrap roads caused the Board to call for monthly rather than quarterly reports on progress. It is recorded that a number of Board members would have preferred someone of wider experience than Billinton to fill the post but overtures to Robert Urie were unsuccessful, he preferring to stay at Eastleigh, (and can one blame him, given the chaotic state of affairs he knew he would have to face?) Thus Billinton came in but even before his formal appointment he was

Cab detail of No 337 at Eastbourne taken undergoing trials in 1913.

instructed to concentrate exclusively on the repair aspect of the work. By this time he was able to take advantage of those improvements in the Works Marsh had at last been able to achieve and his success in meeting the Board's *diktat* was probably a key factor in his obtaining the permanent appointment. At the same time he oversaw the completion of locomotive orders unfinished when Marsh left on sick leave: these were 'H2' no. 426, the sole 'J2' 'Pacific' tank no. 326 – fitted at Billinton's instigation with Walschaerts gear, a Brighton 'first' – and the last ten 'I3's, Nos. 82-91.

  As a further indication that he had carried out the Board's 'repair' remit satisfactorily, between May and December 1913 Brighton put into traffic the first five of the ten-strong 'E2' class 0-6-0T shunting engines. The boilers on these had been ordered by Marsh for fitting to a number of Stroudley 'D1' and 'E1' engines though in the event only 'D1' No. 20 and 'E1' No. 89 received them. (The second batch of five 'E2's, introduced in 1915, had extended side tanks and air-assisted screw and handle reversers.) However, James Jackson, Basil Field's successor in the Chief Draughtsman's Office, had, at Billinton's direction, something much meatier on his drawing board, perhaps the most successful engine to emerge from Brighton Works, the 'K' class 2-6-0 'Mogul'. (Field had been promoted to Works Manager.)

  The main impetus for introduction of this class was provided by Churchward's '4300' 'moguls' which had appeared in 1911. Engines of this wheel arrangement were

used in droves in North America from early in the latter half of the 19th century and proliferated elsewhere as the Victorian era progressed to its conclusion. But it had not found general favour in Britain though UK locomotive builders were, during that same period, happily constructing and shipping such engines particularly to New Zealand and the Cape. The Garstang & Knott End Railway took delivery of a single 2-6-0T in 1870 and Massey Bromley introduced fifteen examples on the Great Eastern in 1878. The design was not his but that of his predecessor, William Adams. They were not particularly successful engines though that was not the fault of the wheel arrangement.

  Two Beyer-Peacock-built 'Moguls' originally bound for Australia had appeared on the Midland & South Western Junction Railway in 1895 and 1897. Moreover, the Great Northern, Great Central and Midland had purchased examples from US builders Baldwin and Schenectady right at the end of the century when a sharp rise in the demand for engines could not be met from national resources.

  Right at the beginning of the 20th century, Dugald Drummond had offered 4-4-0s of classes 'K10' and 'L11'with 5'7" driving wheels for such duties on the South Western though their freight work must have been limited by the adhesion weight available to start such a train and, much more importantly, to stop it. Before him William Adams had introduced his 'A12' class 0-4-2 as a 'mixed-traffic' locomotive. William Dean's GWR 'Aberdares' of 1900 were specifically heavy-haul goods engines but the

No 347 near Arundel on 1 October 1921 with what is likely to be a Three Bridges to Chichester / Portsmouth freight working. The double domed boiler fitted will be noted.   *O J Morris*

Careworn No 2339 on Brighton shed 29 June 1946, with the east side roof of Brighton station in the background. The Weir pump is on the nearside footplating.
H C Casserley

This offside view of a 'K', No (3)2352 through the grime, shows the Westinghouse brake pump. Like no 2339 this engine displays the cutdown mountings to bring it into the composite loading gauge. Note the Ramsbottom type safety valves. Eastleigh, 16 July 1946.

A F Cook

'4300' was a true general-purpose machine that made it a go-anywhere, do (almost!) anything, product. Furthermore the design came at the moment truly mixed-traffic locomotives were being seriously considered as an alternative to those of distinctive nomenclature. Eventually more than two hundred and fifty examples of the class were in GWR service.

The 'pony truck' gave the engine a steadier ride than an 0-6-0 could offer and therefore raised the speed limit at which it could safely travel. That in turn led to larger driving wheels to take advantage of that increased speed potential while the lengthened chassis permitted fitting of a bigger boiler. Nigel Gresley of the Great Northern was the first in the field to follow Churchward's lead, his 'H1' class (later LNER 'K1') coming into traffic in 1912, less than a year after his taking over the Doncaster reins from Ivatt. Gresley did not, however, follow Swindon's lead in providing a coned boiler. Neither did Billinton. But for the first time Brighton turned out an engine with a Belpaire firebox.

The first 'Ks' were laid down alongside the last of the original order of 'E2s', no.337 coming into traffic in September 1913. No. 338 followed in December and the final three of the order appeared at roughly quarterly intervals thereafter, the last, no. 341, emerging some two months after the outbreak of the First World War. These three engines had some modifications incorporated as a result of experience with the first two. Included were alterations to the pony truck control springs to improve the ride and a different blastpipe arrangement, in a smokebox five inches longer than the drawings to minimise fire-throwing, modifications subsequently made to the prototypes. The five engines were then a real success, particularly useful on the heavy military traffic passing through Newhaven, so much so the Government gave authority for construction of five more. Nos. 342-6 were ordered in September 1914 but through the exigencies of wartime did not come into service until two years later.

Some details showed that a number of available parts had been used in the class. For example, the outside 21" x 26" cylinders were the same as on the 'Atlantics', and fitted with the same 10" diameter piston valves driven by Stephenson link motion. First drawings do not show any forward extension of the piston rods but these were fitted though the sandboxes due to be incorporated in the leading splashers were not. The 5'6" diameter 17-spoke driving wheels were as those on the 'E5' tank engines though the coupled wheelbase was six inches longer, and the usual

Ramsbottom safety valves were applied – the later no. 347 uniquely had 'pop' valves - as was the handsome chimney by Basil Field.

The 5'3" diameter boiler incorporated a twenty-one element Robinson superheater of 279 sq ft area and offered, with the firebox, a total heating surface of 1294 sq ft. Pressure was 170psi and the grate area 24.8 sq ft. Tractive effort at 85% of boiler pressure was estimated at 25,103lbs. (The pressure was later raised to 180psi which took the tractive effort up to 26,580lbs.) In working order the engine turned the scales at 63¾ tons of which a most useful 55¼ tons was adhesive. The tender, of a new design with slotted frames though unmistakeably of Brighton pedigree, holding four tons of coal and 3,940 gallons of water, weighed 41½

tons. These were equipped with feedwater heaters which required the engine to be fitted with a Gresham & Craven hot water injector, the clack being mounted on the right-hand side of the firebox. A steam-driven Weir pump was also provided on the left-hand footplate together with Westinghouse brake pump. From the first the engines were provided with carriage steam-heating equipment. The total length over buffers worked out at 57'10". Incidentally, Newhaven shed received a 60' ball-bearing turntable constructed at Brighton in 1917 specifically for these engines.

When new, Nos. 337/8 were finished in red oxide while 1000-mile trials were undertaken. Neither lettering nor numbering appeared other than on the buffer beam. No.

Nos 32351 and 32346 head a most interesting working: a farm removal special on 25 May 1955. Like No 2339 both engines display the cutdown mountings to bring it into the composite loading gauge. Notwithstanding the route code, it is not possible to identify the location / section of line with certainty.

337 was then painted in dove grey lined, lettered and numbered black and white for the official photograph on the Crumbles siding at Eastbourne. But in February 1914, as engines came into service, they appeared in gloss black, lined vermilion. The wartime five were also finished in black but with yellow rather than white numerals.

Perhaps in line with Churchward's preferences Billinton began fitting the class with top-feed apparatus in 1916, nos. 345/6 being the first treated. In this method the clacks were mounted on a manhole set some three feet ahead of the dome. The other three engines of this lot were retro-fitted with this as they went through shops. The second method involved a dome being added on the exact vertical line through the leading driving wheels with the clacks mounted high on its back. No 339 was the first to have this, in February 1920. The object was to deepen the delivery tray and so maximise 'precipitation of solids in the feedwater', (Ellis). (The latter apparatus appeared on boilers among other classes also, specifically two of 'B2x', four 'C3' and six 'C2x'. Inevitably they circulated as engines went for overhaul, and not just among these three classes either.) The dome cover remained in place even when the more conventional method of clacks on the centreline of the boiler's leading ring had superseded top feed. Other minor 'one-offs' were tried out. In 1921 No. 351 was fitted with a Lewis draught regulator which involved an extension to the smokebox and a plain oval chimney and No. 340 had a Worthington feedwater heater and pump added that same year. The Southern later removed all these attachments.

It is believed Billinton contemplated building a tank engine version of the 'K' after the War but the Civil Engineer would not accept it. Thus ten more 'K's were ordered in 1919 following the relaxation of Government controls on material, seven being outshopped in 1920 (Nos. 347-50) and 1921 (Nos. 351-3): all seven were provided with domed top feed from new. The construction of the final three from this order was delayed so that Brighton Works could catch up with the backlog of repairs and maintenance caused by the inevitable difficulties imposed by wartime. But following Grouping and having compared their performance against Urie's 'S15' and his own 'N' class 'Moguls', already earmarked as the Southern's 'standard', Maunsell saw no point in completing the order despite the good showing the class made in terms of ability and reliability and, no less, their excellent riding qualities. The engines were apparently deemed more expensive to run and maintain than their competitors.

Oddly, soon after Grouping three of the class were finished by the Southern in Marsh 'Umber'. From this act a rumour seems to have started and spread intimating that the newly-constituted Southern Board was considering it as the Company's standard for locomotives, though it was more likely to be a means of using up stock while the actual livery was settled upon. For the same reason Eastleigh continued to apply Urie's 'Sage Green' shade to its engines. But in 1924 the Board accepted Maunsell's recommendation to use the slightly darker 'Parsons Green' previously applied by the LSWR only to its coaching stock. In Southern circles thereafter it was known as 'Maunsell Green' and began to be generally used on locomotives from 1925. Despite being essentially mixed-traffic engines the 'Ks' were later all finished in this livery.

Bulleid's arrival changed this. Only the principal main line classes were turned out in the bright Malachite Green while everything else was painted black. The intention had been to make the green more general but shortage of paint prevented this. The changeover was, of course, gradual and a few of the 'K' class retained the Maunsell Green livery almost until the outbreak of the Second World War. Post-Nationalisation the engines, being categorised as 'mixed-traffic', were all finished in BR lined black livery which suited them quite well.

So far as can be ascertained, and despite Maunsell reducing the height of the chimney, dome and the cab roof after Grouping to bring the engines into the 'composite' loading gauge – a fact noted by a small triangle yellow-painted on the front buffer beam above the 'No'- none of the class ever strayed far beyond the Central Division of the Southern Railway or its BR equivalent. Perhaps for that reason there appeared to be no hurry to make these structural changes: No. 351 for example certainly remained unaltered into the early 1930s. The nearest any got to escaping is believed to be occasional appearances at Salisbury on 'through' trains to and from South Wales. (By that time all seventeen had had 2000 added to their numbers, superseding the 'B' that had appeared after Grouping to identify their origin.)

In 1950 a few were temporarily drafted to the Western Section which, because of a shortage of stock for Special traffic to/from the Farnborough Air Show, had borrowed several air-braked ex-GER sets from the Eastern Region. Anecdotal reports suggest these 'foreign' engines became well-liked by local crews despite the shortness of their stay.

At the approaching end of the LBSCR's existence the engines were divided among only four depots with Brighton the stronghold housing eleven examples. Four were on the books at New Cross Gate and one each at Battersea and Three Bridges. Parent sheds had altered little by Nationalisation though Eastbourne had one engine and Fratton two, the remaining fourteen being divided equally between Brighton and Three Bridges. Ten years later Three Bridges had the lion's share with nine while Fratton retained its pair and Brighton shedded the remaining six. (In BR days Fratton shed came under the Nine Elms district, but it had been built and worked jointly by the LBSCR and the LSWR since 1889, though until Grouping there were separate offices and coal stages and designated engine stalls in the roundhouse. It closed officially in November 1959 though stabling went on much longer.)

The 'K' class was complete right to the end of 1962, the first eight at Brighton, the remainder concentrated at Three Bridges. It is evident from the earlier allocations in particular that the engines were rostered for longer distance freight work. These would have been specifically to/from

A Brighton invasion! 'K' class No 32340 and 'E4' 0-6-2T No 32487 (formerly Fishergate) stand outside Ashford Works on 3 July 1960. The cab and mounting will be noted to have been cut down on the 'K'.   *S C Creer*

The really splendid LBSCR gantry at East Croydon lasted until 21st March 1954 when colour-light signalling was introduced south of Norwood Junction. From the left the signals applied to the up local, down local, up main, down main and reversible on which line the train is travelling. The up direction distant signals were worked by / in conjunction with Windmill Bridge Junction box, down direction by East Croydon's South box. The engine is No 2346 working a Norwood to Three Bridges freight.   *H M Madgwick*

the two London yards at Battersea and Willow Walk and the principal staging/sorting points in the south, Brighton itself, Newhaven, Lewes, Hove, Chichester, Horsham and Fratton for example. The interchange yards at Norwood Junction would most certainly have seen them from introduction. I personally regularly recorded them there from early-BR days though it appeared by that time they rarely worked further north: nor, so far as I know, were they ever used on cross-London interchange freight traffic. I also had the very occasional view of one at Wimbledon West Yard right at the end of the 1950s, though Central interdivisional traffic to/ from the Western Section usually involved a 'C2x' or 'Q' which also worked the by-then freight only line to Tooting via Merton Abbey.

At that time also, a 'C2x' was the usual motive power for 'The Morden Milk' but I saw a 'K' on it just the once, at Sutton. What drew my attention was an exhaust note just a little bit different from that produced by a 'C2x' on the climb up the curving 1 in 44/49 'Wall of 'Death' from West Sutton. Derek Cross recalls a conversation on the footplate of one whose driver said quite bluntly 'this engine never slips'. Neither did this one! (A Western Section engineman of my acquaintance said he knew the class as 'Hillclimbers', a deserved nickname.) I can only assume experienced recorders found timing main line trains behind less humdrum locomotives more to their taste. (Incidentally, the headcodes for London Bridge / Willow Walk and Brighton were LBSCR no 1 and 2. A single plain disc below the chimney indicated a routing via Redhill, two plain discs one above the other over the right-hand buffer showed use of the 'Through Line', that is the later 'Quarry' route.)

Until the official curb made in World War One reduced loading on freight trains to 900 tons maximum, these engines were happily taking up to 1000 tons with very little trouble.

Excursion traffic had formed a large part of the Brighton company's earnings almost from its earliest beginnings. Not surprisingly therefore the 'Ks' soon found themselves at the head of such workings, particularly at weekends. But it wasn't just excursions: for the density of passenger traffic from at least the last two decades of the 19th century saw the heaviest freight work taking place late in the day or at night, releasing the 'Ks' for more general rostered passenger duties. There is photographic evidence, for example, of commuter work being undertaken over the main line from London Bridge. Like the 'E5' tank engines, the 'Ks' had a fair turn of speed and though I have not been able to turn up any records of such work 'Brighton in the Hour' non-stop was certainly easily achievable by these engines.

Following withdrawal of all but one of the Brighton 'Atlantics' at the end of summer 1956 the appearance of a 'K' on 'relief' Newhaven boat trains became, if not regular, at least fairly common. They were ideally suited to such work on trains generally loading to between 360 and 400 tons gross, not simply through their pulling power but their proven propensity to gallop when

need be. Derek Cross wrote that... 'they were remarkably good-riding engines which may account for the fact that on the odd occasion when I saw one on a relief express it seemed to be going surprisingly fast'. Contrast that with Bert Hooker's account of a rebuilt 'River' hauling empty stock at 60mph downhill from Buriton towards Petersfield on the Direct Portsmouth when the riding became so rough the fire was quickly vanishing to the front of the grate and the violent hunting made it almost impossible to stand.

Contrast again an event that sticks particularly in my mind, a 'K' in quite filthy condition with twelve London Midland coaches in tow, probably bound for Brighton, haring happily up the 1 in 264 through Thornton Heath with the regulator already all but shut for the 50mph slack at East Croydon despite the short but sharp 1 in 100 to Selhurst still to be surmounted. The Maunsell 'Moguls' that generally powered the Victoria-Brighton trains via Oxted and Uckfield never seemed to have such a relish for their work. Driver Hooker's experience was perhaps reflected there. Certainly, most other 'Moguls', and not only those on the Southern, appeared to be confined to freight traffic or passenger services with frequent stops. (I absolve the LMS 'Crabs' from that statement: they performed very well on express passenger services over the difficult GSWR Carlisle -Glasgow main line via Dumfries.)

Despite three of them having recently received general overhauls, all seventeen engines were withdrawn *en bloc* in the last two months of 1962. More's the pity, for they still had plenty of life in them. (No 32353 was still in steam on 27th December!) But the accountants triumphed over the operators who could have continued to find them work. The timing of the withdrawal proved rather injudicious considering the very severe winter that followed. It is believed at least one example had to be resurrected from its temporary resting place at Hove to assist breakdown gangs working on the catalogue of problems arising from the prolonged freeze. The Bluebell Railway apparently hoped to buy one but with finance concentrated on purchasing the line, could not afford it so, regrettably, none of this unsung, indeed largely unappreciated but most useful and successful class survived the cutters torch. Another class, then, that deserves reincarnation?

Bibliography

Lawson Billinton, A Career Cut Sort, Klaus Marx, The Oakwood Press, 2007.
Robert Billinton, An Engineer Under Pressure, Klaus Marx, The Oakwood Press, 2008.
The London, Brighton & South Coast Railway, C Hamilton Ellis, Ian Allan Ltd., 1960.
History of the Southern Railway, C F Dendy Marshall, rev. R W Kidner, Ian Allan Ltd., 1963 (1982 Reprint).
The Larger Brighton Locomotives, Locomotives Illustrated no. 37, Ian Allan Ltd., Spring 1984.
A Further Selection of Locomotives I Have Known, J N Maskelyne, Percival Marshall, 1962.
Victoria to East Croydon, Vic Mitchell and Keith Smith, Middleton Press, 1987.
Railway Liveries, Southern Railway, Brian Haresnape, Ian Allan Ltd., 1982.
Various edition of The ABC of Southern Locomotives, Ian Allan Ltd., 1942 onwards.

The Twickenham Timeline

The story of Twickenham Station

Nicholas Lewin

Under the auspices of the South Western Railway (est. 1838), the Richmond Railway was opened between Richmond and Nine Elms in July 1846 and extended to Waterloo in July 1848. The Windsor, Staines and South Western Railway then opened the station at Twickenham in August 1848 on the line now extended beyond Richmond to Datchet (extended further to a temporary terminus at Black Potts) and then Windsor itself in December 1849. Although not confirmed, it is possible that Joseph Locke engineered the line with work being contracted to Thomas Brassey.

Twickenham was operated as a semi-terminal station from December 1849 until January 1869, when the Kingston branch was extended to Coombe & Malden (New Malden) and Wimbledon. *Semi-terminal* refers to the fact that trains from Ludgate Hill terminated at Twickenham as well as Kingston. Throughout the history of both the Victorian and post-war stations, service patterns have dictated that Twickenham has always operated as a semi-terminal station. This still happens first thing in the morning and in the latter part of the day.

The various lines promoted in the 1830s & '40s which were absorbed into the South Western Railway, all became known as the London & South Western Railway (LSWR) from 1850.

Later Victorian and Edwardian maps and indeed the 1934 Ordnance Survey map, show Twickenham station as *Twickenham Junction*. So far as can be ascertained, the railway never referred to it as this. [From reference to Network Rail and Southwest Trains sources, the point at which the Strawberry Hill line leaves the Windsor Line is referred to as *Twickenham Junction*, not the station itself. As the up and down lines are physically separated by virtue of being grade-separated, the location of the junction itself is vague in its definition.] Having said all of the above, a recent study of some LSWR publicity reveals that the 1912 map of proposed routes selected for electrification include a station known as *Twickenham Junction* – this is reproduced on page 21 of Riverside Electric (see bibliography). It is highly likely that this is a map produced by contractors/publicists and was not actually published to the public in this form.

As originally built, the station at Twickenham was of a plagiarised tudorbethan design, similar, although larger, to the current stations at Hounslow and Isleworth (originally named *Smallberry Green* when it was the temporary terminus of the Hounslow Loop about a quarter of a mile east of the current station). It is possible that the architect

An 1895 photograph showing a horse-drawn railway van in the station yard outside the main station building on the down side of the line. Of note are the Albany in the background and the cobbled path cutting diagonally across the picture.

91

This photo, dated around 1910, shows a pre-electric railway (without conductor rails or sub-station) but with an enclosed footbridge with the ticket collector's hut just visible above the canopy. The semi-detached railway cottages are clearly visible to the right. The engine appears to be an Adams O2 or T1 on an up train via Richmond.

was Sir William Tite, given the architectural style of his stations all over the LSWR. Early history of the LSWR is notoriously difficult to access. Urban myth has it that the Plans Arch at Waterloo which contained archive material relating to the LSWR was partially damaged during World War II and consequently this early information is no longer available. [It is not an urban myth that Waterloo was damaged by bombs!] Sir William Tite was certainly responsible for some stations on the line from Nine Elms to Richmond, notably Mortlake and Barnes, the latter remaining to this day. These two stations are decoratively much more elaborate than Twickenham and Hounslow were to be, so there remains a question as to whether Twickenham and Hounslow are indeed Tite's work.

Twickenham's original station building (on the down or town side) is likely to have housed the ticket office and waiting room, that being its main *raison d'être*: additionally, porters' offices, lamp rooms, toilets, possibly a telegraph office, and a tobacconist were provided in the same block of structures. Accommodation appears to have been provided (probably for the Stationmaster) on the first floor of the main station building.

The original station layout comprised two platforms, up being No.1 and down No. 2, as is the convention. The station appears to have been built without a footbridge from the outset, with passengers crossing the line on the level at the ends of the platforms – the 1864 map shows no footbridge. Walkways existed at both ends of the station and there was also a staff-only walkway between platform No.1 and No.2 (later No.2 and No.3) until the end of the life of the station – this walkway being roughly midway along the platforms.

It is also just possible that London Road initially crossed the railway on the level. The pointer to this is the age of the single-arch cast-iron bridges which characterise this section of line – of which two remain at Richmond, one at the London end of the platforms and one on the approach to Richmond from St Margarets (near Parkshot). The existing structures are dated 1858 and marked; '*manufactured by Joseph Butler, Stanningley Iron Works nr Leeds 1858*'. It is reasonable to extrapolate that London Road Bridge (as seen in the photographs) also dates from the same time given the huge similarity in design and scale; so what was in place before they were put up? An article that has recently come to light at the Public Records Office at Kew tells us that the construction of the railway severed Old Staten Road in Twickenham. Old Staten Road crossed the railway alignment diagonally and made a flat junction with London Road near the river Crane at a point where London Road was a turnpike. With Old Staten Road cut at its western end (by the new railway) and blocked at its eastern end, a level crossing was provided, it is stated, along with the bridge to maintain access to what is now Brewery Lane on the North side of the railway. Once the steps leading to the old station forecourt were constructed (providing access west of the station) the level crossing was no longer needed and so abolished. But perhaps it is more likely that a level crossing was provided initially for all

users; London Road Bridge may have been built in the late 1850s and with it steps provided to access the station yard? (see below – Kingston, a busier town than Twickenham, originally had two level crossings until such time as the railway authorities realised just what a nuisance level crossings were).

In March 1850, Twickenham gained locomotive servicing and stabling in the form of a single-road brick shed, with turntable and coaling/watering facilities. These had originally been installed at Richmond in March 1846 (when the line terminated there) but were moved to Twickenham as a more logical location (in terms of service pattern). Much of the equipment from Richmond was recovered and reused at Twickenham – certainly the turntable and water tank. The turntable originally filled the limited space between the eastern end of the locomotive shed and the back (north side) of up platform No.1.

In June 1863, the single-road locomotive shed was demolished and replaced with a straight, brick-built, two-road, dead-ended shed with a gable-style tiled roof which incorporated the existing water tank. No images of the engine shed can be found but, from the detail of Kingston shed (albeit a larger facility but from a similar date), this description of Twickenham is likely to be accurate; this is also supported by images of the water tank which remained in situ up to the 1950s. Also in June 1863, the turntable and coaling facilities were moved to their final location sandwiched between the river Crane and where the Strawberry Hill up flyover line was to be located 20 years later.

In July 1863, the branch to Kingston was opened coming off the Windsor line on the level to the west of Twickenham station at *Twickenham Junction*. The covering Act of Parliament was passed in 1859 and only saw the railway extended as far as Hampton Wick and not Kingston itself. The Royal Borough of Kingston was initially not very pro-railway to say the least! The LSWR main line was originally to have passed through Kingston, but such were the objections from the Borough as far back as 1834 when the mainline to Woking was being surveyed, that the (then) London & Southampton routed the mainline through Surbiton - the Directors being "*compelled by the opposition of the town of Kingston*". They did, however, provide a station, known as *Kingston*, close to where Ewell Road crosses the main line near the present Surbiton. That version of Kingston (not really anywhere near its namesake) closed in 1845; even the replacement station to the west (now Surbiton) was called *Kingston* until the 1863 branch arrived at Kingston proper! Anecdotal and minuted evidence supports the theory that Kingston was trying to protect its thriving coaching business. The disagreement between the Town and the monopolistic LSWR was bitter and deep. Even as late as 1879 a deputation from Kingston, including the Mayor, to the LSWR asking for a faster service to London received the following rebuke: "*Kingston compelled the Company to go a mile and a half away from the Town Hall and then as soon as the railway came through Surbiton, Kingston was not satisfied until it had a*

Dating from 1924, an up service (presumably Reading or Windsor) headed by an M7 stands in the platform. Despite the steam motive power the 'juice' rail is in situ. The ticket collector's hut is clearly seen with the end of the footbridge extension on the far right of the photograph. Gas lamps and a horse-drawn vehicle in the station yard belie the date.

station of its own". The Borough's short-sightedness resulted in Kingston forever being served by two branch lines colliding!

Thankfully, when the act for the Kingston branch was passed in 1860, the borough had changed its mind and lobbied the LSWR, requesting that the branch cross the river and terminate at a low-level station in Kingston. Joseph Locke engineered the line, construction of which was contracted to Thomas Brassey. Kingston low-level was known as *Kingston New* or *Kingston Town* during planning and construction to distinguish it from the station on the main line at Ewell Road.

Once open to traffic, the low level terminus was known simply as Kingston and occupied the space roughly where current platform 1 (bay platform) is located and the area of the taxi rank adjacent. Note that, following convention, platform 1 is technically the up platform for trains towards London. The current service pattern makes this seem illogical; the same is true at Teddington.

The branch to Shepperton, which diverged from the Kingston branch on the level at Strawberry Hill, opened in November 1864. The junction itself was originally called Thames Valley Junction. This single-track line was promoted by the Thames Valley Railway Company, incorporated in July 1862 and opened in 1864. The TVR

was a consortium that included the Metropolitan Railway backed by the Great Western. It envisaged a line from Brentford (where both the LSWR and GWR had separate facilities) to a terminus at Chertsey on the north bank of the Thames and so not connecting with the existing LSWR terminus at Chertsey. This was a deliberate move to invade LSWR territory. The consortium promoting the line had had no luck raising capital to build the line and John Aird, the contractor building the railway, looked to extend the line to Weybridge to connect with the LSWR. Aird felt that such an extension would make the Shepperton line more profitable; partially paid in shares, the contractor had a vested interest in the line's success. Although the consortium agreed and parliamentary approval was sought, the LSWR clearly felt threatened and blocked this move too. They felt that the extension could abstract revenue from main line services passing through Weybridge. So it was that the Shepperton branch *"terminated...in a potato field as if weary of going further in such country... a flat and somewhat dreary region of Middlesex"*.

As intended, the TVR was amalgamated with the LSWR in January 1867 through an act of July 1865. Extending the line from Shepperton to Chertsey or Weybridge was again raised in 1885. The idea was dropped for *special* (not defined) reasons. Chertsey Urban District

Council petitioned for the extension to go ahead again in 1906/7 and in 1911/12 no fewer than seven more local authorities also did so; all to no avail. (Perhaps they didn't know that they were being used as political pawns in a game of railway chess, the players of which included the Central London Railway (the Central Line of the future Underground combine) and the LSWR.) By the early twentieth-century, the LSWR probably had no intention whatsoever of extending the Shepperton branch.

Doubling the line to Shepperton was carried out in stages and only completed in 1878. The third arm of the triangle at Strawberry Hill came into being in July 1894, thus enabling a service to run between Waterloo and Shepperton via Kingston as well as via Richmond. However, it was only brought into use for passenger trains in June 1901 – and then only for one evening down service. From the outset users of the Shepperton line have campaigned for faster services to London – even in 1865 trains were taking just short of an hour to cover the c. 19 mile journey compared to 53 minutes via Richmond on the current timetable. Progress? (For clarity; Waterloo to Shepperton via Richmond is 18 ¾ miles and via Wimbledon, 20 ¾ miles.)

After powers were sought in 1866, the Kingston Loop came into being in January 1869 with the opening of the section from the LSWR main line at Coombe & Malden to Kingston high-level. This station is roughly on the site of the current station. From 1869 to 1880 Kingston had both a high-level station and low-level station in use, both of which involved level crossings in accessing them and a steeply graded and curved line linking the two. In 1880, the LSWR rebuilt the stations merging the two concourses and creating one Kingston station (and the Southern Railway did so again in 1935 giving us the station we have today). Doing this removed the level crossings and created the reverse curves between the new station and the river bridge which exist to this day as a vestige of joining the two branch lines to form a through route.

Technically, this new line to Kingston was a separate double-track line to the south of the main line alignment all the way from Wimbledon to Coombe & Malden. As the line connected end-on with the Tooting, Merton & Wimbledon Railway at Wimbledon (currently First Capital Connect/Tramlink platforms and area of the station), the new line to Kingston passed under the main line at Malden in both directions. Not without foresight, the LSWR intended to widen the main line and create the current track plan. So it was in 1884 when the main line became a four-track formation (rather than two separate double-track railways running parallel) that the up and down lines parted company at Elm Road level crossing to form their respective connections with the main line – the unused short tunnel under the main line for the former Kingston up line remains to this day.

Originally there was no station at Strawberry Hill; that came in December 1873 after six years of local

In 1947 a Q1 in dirty Southern black with sunshine lettering is pulling a goods train bound for Nine Elms along the up passenger loop line. Note the cut-back down platform and the replacement of the brick building with a temporary wooden building/platform edge. The condition of the island platform canopy is an indicator of how time is running out for this station. The wartime black / white identification of pillars and other obstructions will be noted.

petitioning by a Mr Freake and Lady Waldegrave who paid a third of the total cost of construction.

From the outset, there appears to have been no formal signal box at Twickenham despite the junction, engine shed and sidings. The 1864 OS map shows an SP (signal post) on the south side of the line near to the junction of the Kingston branch (*Twickenham Junction*). This was probably a signalman's hut or shelter which may or may not have contained levers, with adjacent signals for the junction and possibly point levers adjacent to the point work. In true mid-Victorian fashion it may have been a box structure with the signals on top and levers contained inside, but no evidence has come to light.

The first formal signal-box, known as Twickenham West, was installed in 1884 roughly in the V where the Strawberry Hill up line (the downhill slope of the flyover) joins the up Windsor line. It was a type 2, 2A (built between 1877 and 1884) or type 3 (built between 1884 and 1897) signal-box, and was a conventional LSWR wooden structure probably fitted with Saxby & Farmer (or possibly Stevens & Co.) equipment. Early signal boxes were regarded as moveable or temporary structures, hence the extensive use of timber in construction. This signal box was to last for 63 years…

Complaints about Twickenham station are in evidence as early as June 1873 implying that the station was inadequate for the traffic it was handling even at this time, let alone during the early twentieth-century and its later dilapidation.

The junction of the Kingston branch (*Twickenham Junction*) became grade-separated in October 1883 with the construction of the flyover crossing the Windsor lines for the up Strawberry Hill line. The ironwork of the flyover was to last until 1955 and its steel replacement endures to this day. The first such application of this approach to traffic management by the LSWR, it was to be famously repeated at Hampton Court Junction (for two different lines) and at several other locations on the LSWR network. The grade-separation was required due to the increase in traffic along the line towards Windsor and the potential for congestion with resultant delays where trains crossed on the level with a conflicting movement. This resulted in the up platform No.1 becoming an island platform with two up faces (Nos.1 & 2), whilst old platform No.2 became the solitary down platform, now No.3. Down platform No.3 was 177 metres/585 feet long (eight-car train) and up platforms Nos.1 & 2 were 203 metres/670 feet long and so could accommodate a ten-coach train.

In terms of service pattern to Twickenham, a new facility, creating an additional loop line (the Hounslow Loop) came into use in January 1883 although the Act which formally authorised the round-the-corner link between Whitton Junction and Hounslow Junction was not passed until August of that year.

It is likely that the enclosed footbridge was installed to coincide with the platform alterations around 1883. The pointer to this is the 1864 OS map which has no indication of a footbridge at Twickenham. As originally built the footbridge only linked the two platforms without the later extension to Brewery Lane. It may have been a second-hand structure being reused from elsewhere. The staircase design on down platform No. 3 is unusual with awkward angles and a dark enclosed staircase which exits towards the track and this is what suggests that the bridge may not have been bespoke for Twickenham. Having said that, a photo of a 3-SUB in the first quarter of the twentieth century at Hounslow shows a similarly-designed bridge. The new island platform had a lengthy canopy covering both platform faces, its shape being necessarily asymmetrical due to the curve of the up loop line. The building on the island platform was constructed of timber and, by conjecture, contained offices/storage. There was certainly a small kiosk at the bottom of the footbridge.

The six-road, straight, dead-ended engine shed at Strawberry Hill was built in 1897, replacing and absorbing the facilities at Twickenham, Kingston and Richmond. It was originally known as Fulwell Junction shed. Although Twickenham's second-hand brick shed was demolished, the double brick supports for the water tank (above the entrance to the engine shed) remained until 1954 supplying water to the three LSWR water cranes around the station. Strawberry Hill housed and serviced locomotives for the LSWR suburban services as well as cross-London transfer and other general freights. The shed was expanded in 1907 and its turntable enlarged. Once the goods yards at Feltham began to be developed between 1917 and 1921, Strawberry Hill supplied locomotives for shunting there until Feltham engine shed was built and opened in 1921/2. Feltham consisted of a straight six-road through shed with a saw-edge roof, a 65ft electric turntable, mechanical coaling plant and a single-road repair shop – all closed in July 1967.

The big Urie G16 4-8-0 hump-shunters with their short, sloped, side tanks and the elegant 4-6-2 H16 tank engines are synonymous with Strawberry Hill in their beautifully applied LSWR livery. Other steam locomotive classes shedded at Strawberry Hill included Adams 0395s, 0415s (radial tanks) and T1 & O2 0-4-4 suburban passenger tanks as well as Drummond M7s, 700s and a range of 4-4-0 tender engines. From 1922 Strawberry Hill became an all-electric shed, handling LSWR/SR/BR multiple units thereafter. It was also a rolling-stock commissioning and decommissioning location covering a wide geographical (not just Southern Region) area: Witness a line of Robinson 8K 2-8-0s bound for the Great Western held in the sidings adjacent to the Fulwell Curve; also more recent photographs of EMUs, as well as motor-luggage vans, used as shunting units. For a period during the 1970s and 80s, Strawberry Hill also had elements of research & development work being carried out.

Back at Twickenham station, the extension of the footbridge northwards taking it over the two sidings which had previously been the engine shed, is likely to have taken place fairly soon after closure of the shed. Enabling Rugby supporters easier access to the station on match days, the footbridge extension linked the main station footbridge

Twickenham West – the archetypal Southern Railway art-deco signal box – opened in 1947. Richmond (decommissioned but still standing) is pretty much the same design and size.

directly with Brewery Lane and was controlled by a door adjacent to a ticket collector's hut unlocked on Rugby days.

In 1913 work started on Durnsford Road (Wimbledon) power station. This large steam-driven power station sited where Wimbledon Traincare depot is today, provided traction current for LSWR lines in SW London. A number of different electric traction systems had been evaluated by different railway companies: The LSWR settled on 600 volts DC supplied through the third-rail system that we still have today (although now at a pressure of 750v DC). The first LSWR electric train services started in 1915 from Waterloo – Wimbledon via East Putney.

Electrification came to Twickenham in January 1916 as the Waterloo-Waterloo via Richmond and Kingston services were electrified and along with it the large rotary-converter rectifier station (known simply as a sub-station) sited partly where the engine servicing facilities had been. The apparent delay in electrification was due to the investigation of a complaint from the GPO telegraph division regarding the effects of stray magnetic fields from high-power conductor rails on their (lower voltage) telegraph and telephone network. While Hounslow loop services were electrified in March 1916, services to Windsor remained steam-hauled until July 1930 and those to Reading until August 1938.

The last vestiges of steam locomotive servicing at Twickenham (apart from platform watercranes) disappeared in the 1930s when the turntable was finally removed. The related coaling and storage sidings remained in place as general sidings until 1981; a set of buffer stops remains to this day in the scrub on the north side of the flyover line. The other link to the engine sheds of the past is provided by the two semi-detached cottages still there today. It is

understood that these structures were built by the company for their employees and are located to the east of the substation building.

As we know, the Victorian station at Twickenham was inadequate as early as 1873. Only when the Southern Railway announced plans for its reconstruction in 1925 was serious consideration given to deal with this problem. Their plans were immediately scotched by the Borough of Twickenham communicating its aim to widen London Road Bridge; both schemes would have a direct impact on each other.

By March 1937 a solution was found with financial authority from both the railway and the borough. The new development included an art deco station, located on the east side of a widened London Road Bridge along with implementation of colour-light signalling. Work started in 1938 but was interrupted by World War II. It is possible, although not confirmed, that the design for Twickenham could have been similar to Surbiton. Certainly there is evidence of the present-day layout allowing for greater things; for example, platforms 1 & 2 (installed-as and remaining-as bay platforms) clearly have the potential to be through platforms. Twickenham might have had a station as imposing as Richmond or Surbiton...

There is some evidence that a temporary wood and ash platform was sometimes used to handle rugby crowds. It was sited roughly where platforms 1 & 2 of the current station are today. Although work had started in 1938, there is further evidence that the platforms of the new station were pressed into service after the war prior to its opening.

Down platform 3 of the Victorian station was cut-back at the London end to allow the down line to pass through the southernmost brick arch of London Road Bridge

A 2010 photograph from a similar angle to that taken over a century earlier (see p91). The two key features to spot are the Albany in the background and the cobbled path cutting diagonally across the rough car park – still here some 170 years later – whilst the substation and cottages can be seen in the background.

before slewing over to access the old station. This change involved the demolition of the brick building (porters' office, lamp rooms, etc) on the platform to be replaced with a wooden structure that endured for about fifteen years. The platform structure was cut back and replaced with wooden edging as per the photo on page 95. The resulting reverse curve had a low speed limit as long as this arrangement remained.

Not the least significant of all these confusing developments that were so badly interrupted by the war was Twickenham West signal-box. The new art-deco (*Odeon-style*) box was built in June 1938 as a key component of the scheme to introduce colour-light signalling as far as North Sheen. It seems that the equipment destined for Twickenham West was suddenly redirected to Grove Park (SE London) signal-box when that box burned out in August 1938. Given that the 1884 signal-box at Twickenham was still functioning, and that Grove Park obviously needed urgent replacement in order to get traffic moving again, this unfortunate incident and other priorities during World War II, delayed the commissioning of the new box at Twickenham until 1947.

Some ten years after its outline construction, Twickenham West *Odeon* box, fitted with conventional Westinghouse (successor to Saxby & Farmer) mechanical equipment and boasting an 84-lever frame, opened for business. The art-deco box was to last until Feltham Area Control took over in November 1974.

West signal-box controlled that end of the station as well as the various sidings and loops between the station and, roughly, the flyover. A ground-frame controlled the siding and head-shunt at Marsh Farm Lane (adjacent and on the *country* side of the flyover). This siding initially supplied coal to the Twickenham & Teddington Electric Supply Company's power station at Hamilton Road [closed in the 1950s?]. Latterly the siding served a local coal merchant, J D Firmston of Richmond (who also had facilities at Shepperton) enduring possibly until the late 1970s. (A curiosity, which remains to this day, is a building between White Hart Lane level crossing and Mortlake Station on the south side of the railway line which has the name *Firmston House*.) The ground-frame came under the jurisdiction of Twickenham West and a key was needed for its release. There was a foot-crossing connecting the truncated Marsh Farm Lane (to the south) and its continuation as a footpath to the north, which crossed the two running lines as well as three sidings. Its location on a curve with trains running at appreciable speeds led to several injuries and deaths over the years. Mercifully it is now replaced by a footbridge.

East signal-box (which controlled the goods yard and eastern end of the station throat) was closed in 1938 and replaced with a temporary wooden structure (which in turn was subsumed by the 1974 re-signalling scheme).

During 1949-51 there was frustration that the Victorian station (by now in shabby condition) was still in use and pressure was brought to bear to get the new station completed. The cost of materials had increased considerably since the 1937 scheme had been devised and some materials were in short supply. The newly-formed British Railways re-evaluated the scheme for Twickenham in 1952 and work on the regrettably much-scaled-down brick-and-concrete station that we have today restarted in 1953. The first passengers embarked on their journeys from the new station on 28 March 1954. The old station lingered on but over the next few months was demolished with track being re-aligned, concrete fences erected where once the station had been, and the site cleared generally.

London Road Bridge was finally reconstructed during 1964 almost forty years after the borough's intention to widen the bridge had scuppered the Southern Railway proposal back in 1925. Even in May 1956 the Minister of Transport, asked when the bridge would be widened, responded that he expected Middlesex County Council to submit a scheme for approval during that financial year.

So far as can be ascertained, Twickenham had a mixture of LSWR/SR small wooden name-boards (on the barley-twist platform lamps both at right angles and parallel to the track) and larger running-in boards at the platform ends. The new concrete 1950s station featured illuminated names either as part of the station lighting or the large illuminated running-in boards. Twickenham appears never to have been re-signed by BR in the '50s with the well-known hot-dog type enamel signs. However, a railwayana auction in 2009 featured one of these enamel signs and was referred to as possibly the only one ever made.

The brewery which gave its name to Brewery Lane has an interesting history. Thomas Cole started brewing in Twickenham in 1604 and established a brewery by the river Crane in 1635: However, the building we know as Coles Brewery is likely to date from the mid-1700s. By 1890 it had become Burrows and Coles Brewery. Brandon's of Putney took over Cole & Co in 1892: brewing ceased in 1906. Closed in 1927, the buildings were bought at some point after this by the borough for use as a depot and offices, despite objections from a newly formed Ratepayer's Association. The buildings later succumbed to developers' whims possibly in the 1960s and the site was taken over by the GPO.

Today little remains of the Victorian station west of London Road Bridge, but there *are* telltale signs: the substation building of late Edwardian utilitarian design, the two cottages on the north side of the railway and the scrub land where sidings existed under the flyover and around the old site. (Look closely during the winter and you should see the buffer stop in the undergrowth near the turntable's final site just west of the substation.) The Albany pub is a key landmark that endures. (Looking down from London Road Bridge over the site of the old station (see 2010 photograph opposite), you can still discern the outline of the pavement or boundary of the Victorian station.) Mary's Terrace and the steel footbridge to the east of London Road Bridge are also links to the past.

History is cyclical. In 2013, 140 years after complaints were first raised, Twickenham station is once again the subject of redevelopment. Had the original Southern Railway art deco scheme been implemented, the need to redevelop the station still further in the twenty-first century might not have arisen. Hindsight is wonderful!

I hope that you have enjoyed reading this potted history of a well-known station which somehow never quite made it. I am a member of Twickenham & District Model Railway Club and we have been busy with our rendition of the Victorian station at Twickenham – *Twickenham Junction*. Set in the summer of 1961 to coincide with the inauguration of the Club, our model depicts the grotty station in its twilight years. The track layout is faithful to the 1934 OS map. I continue to research the station's history but find many blind alleys, especially in some of the early history. For example, who was the station architect? Did the LSWR build the cottages and if so when? What more do you know about the pre-1947 signal-boxes located at the west end of the station? Is there anything else *you* can help us with? Please do get in touch either via Kevin Robertson of Noodle Books or direct to me at nrgl@btinternet.com. Thanks in anticipation!

Bibliography

History of the Southern Railway, C F Dendy-Marshall. ISBN 71100059x
The London & South Western Railway vols 1-3, R A Williams. ISBN 71534188X, 0715359401,
Waterloo to Windsor, V Mitchell & K Smith. ISBN 0906520541
Kingston & Hounslow Loops, V Mitchell & K Smith. ISBN 0906520835
London's Local Railways, Alan A Jackson. ISBN 0715374796
London's Disused Stations, vol 5, J E Connor. ISBN 0947699384
Farewell to Southern Steam 1967, C Harris. ISBN 9781857943368
Old OS Maps, sheets 121 & 122 of 1894. ISBN 0850548403 & 0854543983
Rail Centres 17: Clapham Junction, J N Faulkner. ISBN1901945278
Railway World, February 1964, 'The Shepperton Branch of the Southern Region', J N Faulkner
Sunbury, Shepperton and The Thames Valley Railway, K Y Heselton. ISBN 0905178211
Twickenham Past, D Simpson. ISBN0948667222
London's Railways Then & Now, E Course. ISBN 0713452579
Cross Country Routes of the Southern, T Gough. ISBN 0860932672
British Railways Illustrated, vol 19 July 2010. ISBN 09618244
A Railwayman's Recollections of West Twickenham in the 1890s, A Brazier, 1976
The Brewing Industry – a guide to historical records L Richmond / A Turton. ISBN 0719030323
London, Kent, Surrey & Dorset steam, M Welch. ISBN 1854142143, 1854142380, 1954142798,
Southern Steam in Action, Nos 2, 3 & 4 – Bradford Barton. ISBN 0851531962, 085153290x, 0851533167
Twickenham: Economic and social history, A History of the County of *Middlesex: Volume* 3: (1962), pp. 151-155. URL: http://www.british-history.ac.uk/report.aspx?compid=22291 (Coles Brewery)
Guildford via Cobham, H Mallinson. ISBN 0954393422
The Southern Way (various issues, K Robertson) Noodle Books
The Riverside Electric, Colin Chivers, 2010. ISBN 0950374156 (South Western Circle Monograph #5, 2010)
http://hew.org.uk/?q=system/files/IndustrialHeritageTalkWithImages.pdf
(History of Hamilton Road power station, Twickenham by C Cooper)
Backtrack & Railway Magazines
BR working timetable *London West Suburban* 1949
Photos from Roger Carpenter and the brothers Blencoe
The Southern Railway Group & The South Western Circle.

Terry Cole's Rolling Stock File No. 25
In Colour

Coaches from each of the three Southern constituent companies feature this time offering a comparison between the differing company styles.

Above - *Here we have two ex-London and South Western Railway coaches which, having finished their revenue earning days, have been converted for use with breakdown trains and painted in bright red departmental livery. Notice the two different styles of LSWR guard's lookout. The left hand one is a 4-compartment Corridor Brake Third DS3198, formerly SR 3161 to Diagram 134, converted in 1952. It was built in 1921 and was 57ft long by 8ft 6in wide excluding lookouts. The right hand vehicle is 4-compartment Non-Corridor Brake Third DS3210, formerly SR 2956 to Diagram 124, converted in the early 50s and having acquired the underframe of sister coach 2960. It was built in 1907 and was 56ft long by 8ft wide excluding lookouts. Both vehicles were based at Dover as branded here but later saw service at Nine Elms from where they were withdrawn in March 1964. [With thanks to Mike King for identification and information on these two vehicles.]*

Opposite top - *This shows Special Traffic set No 389 in Maze Hill sidings. The date is probably the summer of 1958 as the set is in BR green livery rather than crimson and cream. The Southern maintained a considerable number of such sets for use in the peak excursion period even if they only made a handful of trips a year, something that was swept away as the 50s ended. Nearest the camera is a Corridor Tricompo Birdcage Brake, probably No S6629S which with S6628S was allocated to this set at the time. These were from a batch of 15 similar coaches (to three slightly different designs) built by the South Eastern & Chatham Railway at Ashford in 1907. Designed for through services to other companies, they included separate compartments for 1st, 2nd, and 3rd class passengers. The 3rd class accommodation was located next to the guards van in two compartments with a toilet in between. 1st and 2nd passengers had their toilet at the far end of the coach so did not need to mix with the lower orders. The next vehicles in the set are ex-SECR corridor thirds. Set 389 was withdrawn in early 1959. [See also Rolling Stock File No1]*

Hauled by the Brighton Works 'Terrier' replete in LBSCR livery is ex LBSCR Push – Pull set 650 in use for an enthusiasts' special at Kemp Town, Brighton on 3 November 1956. Nearest the camera is Driving Brake Composite No S6940S. This was originally built for the overhead electric services but was never used, instead being converted to Push-Pull operation in 1931 and retaining the characteristic large end windows. Its partner vehicle is ex-LBSCR 48ft third No S2087S which was fitted with a new underframe by the Southern to see further service. The set is resplendent in British Railways Crimson Lake livery. It was withdrawn in August 1959.

[All photos Terry Cole Collection]

The Terry Cole Colour Files
The Southern in the Fifties and Sixties

The Southern alone among the 'Big 4' companies spent much of its time effort and money into extending its electric network. This meant that it still had a very diverse fleet of steam locomotives operating in the 1950s. These pictures, taken in the fifties aim to show some of that diversity.

These four photos were all taken at Waterloo on the same day c 1958

Here Schools class 30907 'Dulwich' in BR lined black and still carrying the early crest waits with a train for Southampton Terminus.

H16 No 30516 shunts a Maunsell Restaurant Car in red and cream livery out of the station.

Urie H15 No 30486, built 1914, runs into the station to collect empty stock. The loco is in BR lined black livery with the later crest which it received in June 1957. No 30486 was the only Urie H15 to receive the later crest and it was withdrawn in July 1959. In the background is an electric multiple unit made up of rebuilt LBSCR vehicles.

King Arthur No 30450 'Sir Kay' waits to leave Waterloo light engine. Behind can be clearly seen the guard's door and ducket of the LSWR 'Ironclad' brake of set 442. No 30450 was withdrawn in September 1960.

D No 31574 has arrived at Redhill with a Tonbridge, Guildford and Reading line train in May 1956. Behind the locomotive is one of the SECR 'Birdcage' sets. No 31574, one of the last survivors of the class, had little time left to run, being withdrawn in October of that same year.

R1 No 31337 is waiting at Folkestone Harbour station. The presence of a bowler hatted official talking to the driver and what are probably enthusiasts on the right suggest this may be a special train. The coach behind the loco is one of Maunsell's 'Nondescript' brakes. No 31337 was withdrawn in February 1960.

L class No 31768 is seen here on Faversham shed on 10th March 1957. The Ls were a common sight on the South Eastern section in the 50s but all had gone by December 1961, No 31768 being one of the last.

Ex LBSCR K class Nos 32353 and 32351 await their next turn of duty at Three Bridges shed. The K class succumbed to the wholesale cull of the remaining older Southern locomotives, all 17 being withdrawn en bloc at the end of 1962

Brighton Atlantic No. 32424 'Beachy Head', the last of its class, has failed with a hot big end at Horsted Keynes whilst working the LCGB Southern Counties Ltd railtour on 24th February 1957. The locomotive was repaired and continued working until April 1958.

This line-up of locomotives awaiting cutting up at Ashford works was taken in early 1960. Leading the line is R1 No. 31337 followed by O1 No. 31370, an H, C2X and an SECR 4-4-0. Carriage underframes are in the foreground. All images Terry Cole Collection.

Engines being prepared for the road at Ashford. On the right one of the crew tightens the smokebox door 'dogs' on U1 31902. Behind is a Schools class. On the left a C class is being oiled up. 31902 was withdrawn in November 1962. The last C class lasted in traffic until mid 1963. All images Terry Cole Collection.

Looking east from Ford Junction on the line towards Littlehampton. The train approaching (a local goods?) has left Littlehampton, next stop Ford. On the extreme left is the west curve of the triangle taking the Mid-Sussex line from the coastway route north-east towards the present day Arundel station and on to Pulborough. In the distance and linking the two operational railways, is the 1887 connection allowing trains to run direct between Littlehampton and Arundel without the need to reverse at Ford. In the foreground identified by the pole-route, is the original alignment of the 1846 part of the coastway route, disused since 1887.

(EARLY) CLOSED LINES - 1
Ford to Lyminster

We are delighted to introduce the first of an occasional feature on long-forgotten Southern area lines - and not those closed by a certain 'Dr'! Instead these are routes which were deemed superfluous decades before, but which route might still be traced years ago.

The original railway between Ford and what was then called Littlehampton & Arundel station (situated in the parish of Lyminster), opened in stages in 1846. From Worthing in the east the, route reached Lyminster, 18 miles from Brighton, on 16 March 1846. Continuation west through Ford as far as Chichester took place on 8 June 1846. As the names imply, 'Littlehampton & Arundel' was then the nearest station for the two locations, although Arundel gained its own station consequent upon the opening of the Mid Sussex route on 3 August 1863 and Littlehampton, when the railway was extended to the seaside town on 12 August 1863. The junctions for both the Arundel and Littlehampton lines faced west at Ford Junction, meaning through running from the direction of Worthing and Littlehampton was not possible without a reversal at Ford Junction. A similar situation existed for trains from Arundel destined for Littlehampton which also had to reverse at Ford Junction. With the opening of separate stations at Arundel and Littlehampton proper, the former 'Littlehampton & Arundel' stopping place was closed in 1863. (The original name was simply Littlehampton it was renamed Littlehampton and Arundel in May 1850).

This arrangement persisted for 20+ years after which the LBSCR decided improvements were necessary. These came in the form of a chord to make a triangle between the Arundel and Littlehampton lines and so allow for through running from the latter location eastwards to and from Worthing. At the same time the route between what was deemed Arundel Junction (the north end of the triangle)

At the opposite end of the abandoned line, the course may be seen veering off left. To the right the railway continues on to Arundel Junction. Lyminster level crossing was behind the photographer.

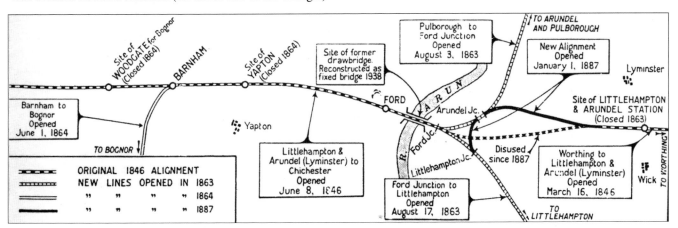

and the line towards Worthing was given a new alignment. Both the chord and new alignment opened on 1 January 1887, in which year the original section from Ford Junction closed.

Almost 85 years ago, on 26 September 1929,

Edward Wallis visited the location and recorded the accompanying images. With the track long gone it was surprising the pole route still complete with wires remained, and was presumably still in use for railway purposes.

Along the trackbed of the abandoned section of line.

Left *- Looking east.*

Bottom - *Looking west.*

The length of route abandoned , and ditto the length of the new alignment, were both in order of two miles.

Opposite *- two views of the former 'Lyminster' station. Both looking west. (The main building was on the south side). Lyminster Crossing signal box, controlling the level crossing of the same name, may just be glimpsed in the right distance of the top view.*

All were taken on 26 September 1929 by Edward Wallis - courtesy David Wallis.

Having perhaps not given our letters pages sufficient priority in the last few issues, a promise was made to undertake some catching up. So without further ado:

From Jeremy Clarke re SW23, "Another for the pot! The upper picture on p101 of *'Tangmere'* can be a little more detailed. The engine was turned out of Brighton in September 1947 as part of Order No 3213. In the photo it retains its Southern Malachite Green livery though 'British Railways' appears in full on the tender. The engine still carries its SR number albeit with an 'S' prefix, but as yet is without either a shedplate or numberplate on the smokebox door. The No 17 headcode indicates the train is for Ramsgate, travelling via the Chislehurst spur to the ex-LCDR line at St Mary Cray Junction and then Chatham and Faversham. This ties in with the number 469 on the disc, a Ramsgate duty, indicating the engine is probably working home on an evening rush-hour service. There is plenty of light still streaming into the station so obviously not winter, more likely then, all things considered, to be late-Spring 1948. I cannot say for sure which train this is but suggest it will be fast to either Chatham or Faversham, perhaps even first stop Whitstable as the 17.14 was for some years."

Also from Jeremy reference his recent article on the Brighton 'Atlantics': "Subject: Brighton to Bournemouth and return on an H2. Ever since I received SW23 and saw this extra piece I have become convinced I've read it before, many years ago. Who wrote it now escapes me, if I ever bothered to notice, but the writing style is definitely familiar. Definitely not from one of the usual suspects though, Allen, Nock, Semmens, Cross etc. The 'Net' has not produced anything useful yet either, which leads me to believe I saw it in one of the several railway magazines of the past, very probably 'Railway World' or perhaps 'Trains Illustrated' in its original small format. Will continue digging….." *(We found this as a very old set of sheets of paper reminiscent of an old photocopier. Size wise the paper was A5 so would certainly fit in with one of the early magazines. Unfortunately there was nothing to indicate the origins - Ed.)*

Another of Jeremy's articles has elucidated the following from John Burgess, "I too acquired a remaindered copy of Ian Allan's reprint of the LSWR 1909 Working Timetable, at 20/- an even better bargain than Jeremy Clarke's copy, although I am slightly disappointed that the reduced price is scrawled in biro rather than fountain pen. It therefore made sense to refer to the timetable whilst reading the article, and I may be able to help with a couple of Jeremy's queries.

The 9.40 a.m. Windsor to Guildford service which is marked as No.176 between Byfleet Junction and Woking continues on page 201 as No.27, where it arrived at Guildford at 10.47 a.m. As Jeremy notes, its timings between Windsor and Woking are listed under the Windsor lines group (page 242, No.17).

The 'Special with Discharged Soldiers As Required' from Fort Brockhurst at 11.38 a.m. continued from Fareham along the Meon Valley line as No.4 on page 125 to Waterloo, where it arrived at 2.03 p.m. The timings from Alton to Wimbledon are set out on page 77, No.247. From Wimbledon it ran via East Putney, and here the timings are set out on page 90 of the Metropolitan District timetable, No.230. There is a 5 minute stop at Clapham Junction and a note which reads 'Detach Carriages at Clapham Junction for Northern Companies Lines; if punctual precede No.231 Up.' This and a stop at Vauxhall are the only scheduled station stops on the entire journey. All very different from contemporary train services.

Another service from the timetable which I find fascinating is that between Ash and Aldershot, set out in a timetable for services between Farnham, Aldershot, Guildford and Shalford Junction. The original SER line from Redhill to Reading opened in 1849, on the same day as various LSWR lines in the Guildford area including the Guildford to Farnham via Tongham line. However, Aldershot did not get its own services until 1870 when the LSWR opened the line from Pirbright Junction, and a spur was constructed from this line to enable direct services from Aldershot to Guildford with running powers over the SER Reading line from Aldershot South Junction to Ash Junction where the Tongham line diverged. (Shalford Junction to Ash Junction was an LSWR line over which the SER exercised running powers).

In 1879 the SER obtained reciprocal running powers over the spur into Aldershot, and in February 1909 started a fairly intense local service using P class 0-6-0Ts and ex-LCDR 4-wheel pull-push fitted stock between Ash

sincerely, John Burgess". *John - thank you, I know they will be appreciated and not just by me - KR.*

Now for a fascinating comment from Pat Bell on the topic of SR Brake Vans: "Most interesting articles. M360327 ended its days broken up at Woking C&W with a 1930s era 25T van after they were involved in an accident at Aldershot involving a ballast cleaner. The same incident resulted in two of the Aldershot p/way gang being badly injured, Sid Edmonds and 'Appy' Appleton - I wish I could remember the year - late 1970s probably.

The prewar and wartime builds made an interesting ontrast. Wartime build used concrete poured into the underframe as ballast, the prewar used scrap iron (broken tools, off-cuts, etc) including the pin in the photos. Could this be the last mortal remains of Adams 'Jumbo' No 515?

and Aldershot. The locomotives were based at Ash shed ,which was a Reading subshed and which dated from 1856. Both LSWR and SECR services between Ash and Aldershot are fully set out in the 1909 timetable, the SECR trains being in their first year of operation. There were no less than 21 weekday passenger services each way run by the SECR compared with six LSWR weekday passenger services each way, most of which ran to and from Guildford. In addition, the SECR ran four goods trains into Aldershot with two returns out of Aldershot, no LSWR goods services appearing in the timetable. Four of the LSWR services in each direction are identified as Motor services. From this, it might be thought that the Aldershot line belonged to the SECR rather than LSWR!

The P class did not last long on the services as loadings increased. From about 1919, they were replaced by R or R1 class 0-4-4Ts. By this date, the original 4-wheel sets had been replaced by four ex-LCDR bogie coaches, and if all four were in use this was too much for the P class engines. The LCDR bogie sets (which ran until 1936) were the last of this company's coaches to remain in mainland service, although several survived on the Isle of Wight until 1948.

The services continued into the SR period until 1937, when the route from Aldershot to Guildford was electrified, and the service pattern altered to run between Aldershot and Guildford. The Tongham branch was an immediate casualty of this event, with passenger services ceasing on the same day that the electric units started running.

I attach a couple of my paintings, the first showing a wartime scene at Ash with the Aldershot shuttle headed by a P class 0-6-0T waiting in the bay platform while an O class 0-6-0 runs through with a freight, and the second showing a later SR scene with an R class 0-4-4T hauling a train of LCDR bogie coaches over the Basingstoke Canal just before reaching the spur at Aldershot South Junction. Yours

Now from Derek Taylor at South Eastern Trains. "Following on from correspondence that started in SW19 regarding level crossings, I heard that Stone Crossing may soon be replaced by a bridge . I have taken a trip there and attached are three images. The frame is dated 1938.

John Lacey adds a useful comment on SW22, "Re-reading Southern Way 22 I noticed a picture of "Jones Furniture Store" in bomb damaged state at Southampton. The store name would be "Edwin Jones" but the "Edw" part has gone."

A question from Tony Francis, Fleet Standards Engineer, Southern Railway, "I was interested In Mike King's article 'More Brits - and other BR Standards' featured in Southern Way Issue 23 as the picture of 70014 *"Iron Duke"* at Maidstone East is the only image I've seen of one of the Stewarts Lane 'Britannias' not taken on BTR 1, the route via Orpington and Tonbridge. Does any reader have any record that shows either 70004 or 70014 worked via the BTR 3 route via Chatham? My father, who was fireman at Faversham, thinks that he can recall seeing either 70004 or 70014 passing Herne Bay on a summer weekend on its way from Victoria to Ramsgate, which would suggest that they occasionally did turn up on the odd non-boat train working. As I was born, bred and still live in Faversham, I'm particularly interested! Regards – and thanks for a really interesting read."

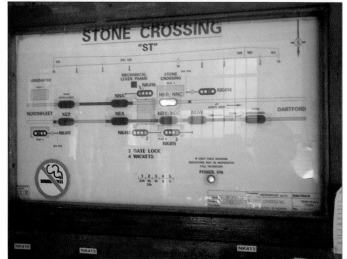

We passed Tony's query to Mike King who answers as follows, "An interesting question and one that I cannot answer positively. I have looked through a number of books and articles but cannot find a picture of a "Brit" on the Chatham route at all. Someone who might know would be Dave Larkin (lives in Albion Court, Albion Road Sutton - not sure of the exact address) as he is modelling Gravesend Central and he remembers it in the 1950s so would have taken note of such locos - he recalls original Merchant Navies coming through with diverted boat trains at that time but I do not recall him mentioning Brits as being on the line - not that they would have come through there on the usual Dover via Chatham boat trains as these would have normally gone over Sole Street to/from Rochester Bridge. If a "Packet" was allowed through, then I cannot see why a "Brit" would not be passed for the route.

Obviously 70004 was "bulled up" for the "Arrer" so would be the favourite loco if available, leaving 70014 to be rostered for other duties once it was known that "Will" would be on duty. No doubt R. H. N. Hardy would have the answer so maybe one to put in the letters page." *(If anyone can help we will pass on the information - Ed.)*

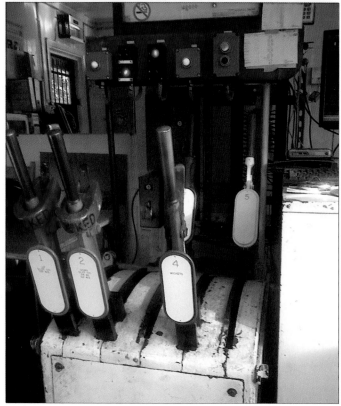

More now from Jeremy Clarke, and this time 'comments upon the comments'. "Hi Kevin. I've only now got as far as 'Rebuilt' and note Richard Bell's comments on the location of the 1927 crash at Dunton Green. I accept what he says as his statement is apparently taken from the Inspector's Report. But there clearly is some discrepancy somewhere. The fireman is reported as stating he 'heard knocking' soon after the engine left Polhill tunnel, believed to be the leading drivers off the road and hitting the chairs. Now, if *'River Cray'* were derailed there, as the knocking seems to indicate at first sight, the engine travelled for nearly two miles 'off the road' before the crash. So far so good. But were that so, it passed successfully through all the pointwork at Dunton Green station before coming to grief. Unlikely I think: therefore it appears equally unlikely the knocking was the sound of a derailed engine. So what was it? Who knows? Ah, but perhaps 'River Cray' had been derailed after Polhill. Did it by chance rerail itself shortly afterwards and then, maybe, become derailed for a second time at Dunton Green, perhaps as it passed over the pointwork there? Another possible point of confusion is that, although Shoreham Lane does

indeed cross the line south of Dunton Green, Filston Lane, which bridges it north of that station and about 800 yards south of the tunnel exit, is often referred to locally as Shoreham Lane because it provides another and more direct link between that village and Dunton Green. Its bridge does not have a centre pier now and, of course, may never have done so, neither does the line run into a cutting until some 60 chains beyond it. All very puzzling though one cannot gainsay an official report of course. Intriguing though?"

Top - *We were recently passed three images taken at dinners / presentations. Unfortunately all are undated. We feel we should be able to recognise some at least - suggestions would be welcome....*

Bottom - *Amazing what there is still to find. Alan Wickens rescued this poster a few years ago when the owner of a hostelry in Llangollen decided to close up.*

REMEMBER FULLERTON?

Remember Fullerton? I am sure that, like me, that many do. On the erstwhile Andover to Romsey section of the Andover to Redbridge route - the section south of Romsey survives - the railway from Andover, through Clatford, Fullerton, Stockbridge, Horsebridge and Mottisfont succumbed to closure from 7 September 1964. Opened in 1865, the course had followed that of a disused canal and had even at one time been the projected route of a broad gauge line for the GWR to reach Southampton. Instead it was LSWR from the outset, with a junction provided at Fullerton in 1885 when a connection was made with a short line from Hurstbourne through Wherwell and Longparish. The line from Hurstbourne was never a financial success (it was built as a means of enticing the Didcot, Newbury & Southampton to cease construction south of Whitchurch and instead reach Southampton by means of running powers over the LSWR west and then south west from Whitchurch. With no connection ever provided between the two railways at Whitchurch it was not surprising the Hurstbourne - Fullerton section was of little use and, having been singled in 1913, it closed in 1931).

The main line south of Andover fared rather better for apart from a reasonable through service - the intermediate stations could hardly be expected to generate much traffic - it was also the route of choice for services to and from the MSWJ at Andover. However with the closure of the MSWJ in 1961 and road competition it was now only a matter of time. Even so there was a brief episode of diesel workings in the latter years.

The remains at Fullerton were captured by Stephen Duffell in 1969, at which point all was intact but had remained moribund for some time. (Demolition did not take place until some time after closure.) The photographs show the extensive facilities that once existed, including the former space occupied by the platforms for the Hurstbourne line - opposite top - and on this page, the original 'Fullerton Bridge' station disused since 1885 when the 'new' station was provided on a site slightly further south.

Hard to imagine that it was here that passengers might once have used Fullerton to change trains and that an LSWR steam-railmotor had operated a circular Andover - Whitchurch - Hurstbourne - Fullerton - Andover service. During WW2 there was even the regular working of an 'office coach' from Southampton Central every night. This was stabled at Fullerton during the hours of darkness and worked back first thing in the morning, the idea being to keep important papers safe from the risk of bombing at Southampton.

We are extremely grateful to Stephen for submitting these (and a few more) views. *Please,* if you have a favourite and there are a few slides as well, we would love to include them.

(More on Fullerton in its heyday, which make for an interesting comparison with the views seen here, will be found in our recently published book 'Southern Infrastructure'.)

Geographic Bias in The Southern Way Magazine

Alan Postlethwaite

	Area	SE&CR	LB&SCR	L&SWR	Wight	Total
A	Number of Pages	406	499	1019	58	1982
B	Pages %	21%	25%	51%	3%	100%
C	Route Miles	638	457	1029	54	2178
D	Route Miles %	29%	21%	47%	3%	100%
E	Bia (B-D)%	-8%	+4%	+4%	0	0

Notes:

1. Twenty-five issues of *The Southern Way* were included in the survey (Nos. 0 to 24).
2. The total number of magazine pages was 2738 of which 756 were neutral (28%).
3. Purely SR or BR subject matter was treated as neutral.
4. Each area includes independent railways such as Longmoor, Selsey and the KE&SR.
5. Joint locations are split equally between the owning companies.
6. Dual material is also split equally eg a Brighton train in a South Western location.
7. The route miles are taken from Tony Goodyear's article on the SR in SW8 (page 68).

The L&SWR has the greatest number of pages because it has the greatest route mileage. The bias of 4% towards the L&SWR is less than expected but the bias of 4% towards the LB&SCR is more than expected. The heavier bias of 8% against the SE&CR was expected. The reasons for these biases are not understood. The ingredients of the SE&CR are much the same as for the L&SWR and LB&SCR but fewer SE&CR railwaymen and enthusiasts have put pen to paper.

An accounting challenge - a South Western engine shunting Brighton and Chatham coaches at Ventnor.